George Abbot
Archbishop of Canterbury
1562–1633
A Bibliography

GEORGE ABBOT
Archbishop of Canterbury
1562–1633
A Bibliography

RICHARD A. CHRISTOPHERS

Assistant Keeper in the Department of Printed Books

British Museum

Published for
THE BIBLIOGRAPHICAL SOCIETY OF
THE UNIVERSITY OF VIRGINIA

THE UNIVERSITY PRESS OF VIRGINIA
CHARLOTTESVILLE

PREFACE

This bibliography was originally compiled in
part fulfillment of the requirements of
Part II of the examination for the Academic
Post-Graduate Diploma of Librarianship of
the University of London, and I am very
grateful to Professor Raymond Irwin, director
of the School of Librarianship, both for
supervising the original work and for giving
permission for it to be published by the
Bibliographical Society of the University of
Virginia.

I should also like to thank for their help
and encouragement Professor Arthur F. Stocker
and Mr. John Cook Wyllie of the University of
Virginia and the staffs of all the libraries
in which I have worked, particularly those
who have so promptly answered my many letters
and shown a personal interest in my work.

R. A. Christophers

Bramley, Surrey

1965

CONTENTS

SYMBOLS AND ABBREVIATIONS

A   LIBRARIES AND OTHER LOCATIONS

The symbols given below are based on the system established by D.G. Wing.

L	British Museum.
LG	Guildhall Library.
LLP	Lambeth Palace.
LS	Society of Antiquaries.
LU	London University.
LUC	University College, London.
LW	Dr. Williams's Library.

BR	Bristol Reference Library. (By letter.)
C	Cambridge University Library.
CE	Emmanuel College, Cambridge.
CH	Henry Huntington Library, San Marino. (microfilm at Bodleian Library, Oxford)
CT	Trinity College, Cambridge.
CU	Chicago, Newberry Library. (By letter.)
DM	Archbishop Marsh's Library, Dublin.
DN	National Library of Ireland, Dublin.
DT	Trinity College Library, Dublin.
DU	Durham University. (By letter.)
GuA	Abbot's Hospital, Guildford.
GuPL	Guildford Public Library.
LC	Library of Congress. (Printed catalogue.)
MnU	Minnesota University Library, Minneapolis. (By photocopy.)
O	Bodleian Library, Oxford.
OB	Balliol College Library, Oxford. (By letter.)
WF	Folger Shakespeare Library, Washington. (Photocopy of catalogue in the North Library, British Museum.)
Y	Yale University Library, New Haven, Conn. (By letter.)
C-	Cambridge, England.
D-	Durham, England.
E-	Edinburgh.
L-	London.
O-	Oxford.

-C	Cathedral Library.
-PL	Public Library.
-U	University Library.

B   MAJOR WORKS CONSULTED

All were published in London unless otherwise stated.

Arber   Arber, E., ed. A transcript of the
                    registers of the Company of Stationers
                    of London, 1554-1640. 1875-94.
                    [No. 114.]
BB   Biographica Britannica. v. 1. 1747.
                    [Article on Abbot.] [No. 156.]
Thomason   British Museum. Catalogue of the
                    pamphlets ... relating to the Civil
                    War ... collected by George Thomason.
                    1908.
                 British Museum. Catalogue of the
                    printed books. 1881-1904, 1931- .
SPD   Calendar of state papers, domestic
                    series. (1601-34) 1859-97.
                 Davies, G. Bibliography of British
                    history, Stuart period, 1603-1714.
                    1928.
DGK   [Deutscher Gesamtkatalog.] Gesamt-
                    katalog der preussischen Bibliotheken.
                    v. 1. Berlin, 1931.
DNB   Dictionary of national biography. v. 1.
                    1885. [Article on Abbot.] [No. 168.]
                 Dr. Williams's Library. Catalogue of
                    the library [and supplements]. 1841- .
WF(c.e.)   Folger Shakespeare Library. Photocopy
                    of Folger catalogue in the North
                    Library, British Museum.
Gerould   Gerould, J.T. Sources of English
                    history of the seventeenth century ...
                    in the University of Minnesota
                    Library. Minneapolis, 1921.
                 Guildford Public Library, Reference
                    department. Catalogue of works in
                    the library relating to the county
                    of Surrey. Guildford, Eng., 1957.
                 Historical Association. Annual bulletin
                    of historical literature.
                    1911 to date.
                 House of Commons Library. A
                    bibliography of Parliamentary debates
                    of Great Britain. 1956.

International bibliography of historical sciences. 1916 to date.

Johnson
Johnson, A.F. A catalogue of engraved and etched English titlepages down to ... 1691. 1934.

Lancaster, J.C. Bibliography of historical works issued in the United Kingdom, 1946-1956. 1957.

LC(c.e.)
Library of Congress. A catalog of books ... issued to July 31, 1942 [and supplements]. Washington, 1942 to date.

McK.
McKerrow, R.B. Printers' and publishers' devices ... 1485-1640. 1913.

McK. & F.
McKerrow, R.B., and Ferguson, F.S. Titlepage borders ... 1485-1640. 1932.

Madan i
Madan, F. Oxford books. v. 1, The early Oxford Press. Oxford, 1895.

Madan ii
Madan, F. Oxford books. v. 2, The Oxford literature, 1450-1640 and 1641-1650. Oxford, 1912.

STC
Pollard, A.W., and Redgrave, G.R. A short-title catalogue of books printed in England ... 1475-1640. 1926.

Ramage
Ramage, D. A finding list of English books to 1640. Durham, Eng., 1958.

Revue d'histoire ecclésiastique. Louvain. From 1939 to date.

Royal Historical Society. Writings on British history, 1934-45. 1937-60.

Russell
Russell, J., ed. The life of Dr. George Abbot. Guilford, 1777. [No. 157.]

Russell, T. Interleaved copy of Russell's life of Abbot with MS notes. GPL - "Russell notebook, 5."

Russell, T. MS extracts from books on Abbot. GPL - "Russell notebook, 4."

Russell, T. MS text of most of John Russell's life of Abbot with additions. GPL - "Abbot book."

Society of Antiquaries. Catalogue of a collection of printed broadsides. 1866.

McAlpin Cat.
Union Theological Seminary, New York. Catalogue of McAlpin collection of

	British history and theology. New York, 1927-30.
Watt	Watt, R. Bibliotheca Britannica. 1824.
Welsby	Welsby, P.A. George Abbot. 1962. [No. 183]
	Welsby, P.A. Lancelot Andrewes. 1958. [No. 182]
Williams' Index	Williams, F.B. Index of dedications, etc. before 1641. 1962.
Wing	Wing, D.G. Short-title catalog of books printed in England ... 1641-1700. New York, 1945-51.
Wood	Wood, A.à. Athenae Oxonienses. 1692. [No. 147.]

C MISCELLANEOUS

< >	Square brackets in text.
*	Important entry; used in Appendix only.
+	Printer or publisher of Abbot's work only after his death; used in Index C only.
a, b	Recto, verso.
B.L.	Black letter.
c.e.	Catalogue entry transcribed or information sent by post.
comp.	Compiled, compiler.
ed.	Edited, editor.
e.t.p.	Engraved titlepage.
f., ff.	Folio, folios, or following.
m.f.	Microfilm.
n.	Note.
p., pp.	Page, pages.
r.t.	Running title.
$	Signatures; used for reference to whole gatherings or, when followed by letter and number, for page references in notes if pages not numbered.
t.p.	Titlepage.
trans.	Translated, translator.
v., vols.	Volume, volumes.
x.	Copy not seen; prefixed to entry number.

INTRODUCTION

A   BIOGRAPHICAL NOTE

     An Archbishop of Canterbury will inevitably
attract some attention in histories of his period however undistinguished his primacy, since by virtue of
his office, in the seventeenth century at least, what-
ever his inclinations he could not help being in the
forefront of political life. Probably among the most
enthusiastic of his chroniclers will be those writing
of his birthplace, and through these I became inter-
ested in George Abbot, who, born, educated and buried
at Guildford, Surrey, and retiring there when affairs
of state weighed too heavily upon him, has left his
mark upon the town in the form of the hospital which
he founded, two schools named in his honour, and a
romanticized general impression of him typified by the
inscription outside the Hospital of the Blessed
Trinity "Born a poor Guildford boy & became Archbishop
of Canterbury".

     From Guildford and its Grammar School Abbot
proceeded to Balliol College, Oxford, and rose through
the Schools to Doctor of Divinity and Master of
University College in 1597. He appears to have been
well liked by his pupils and for them wrote his
Geography, of which I give details in entries 3-16.
This was indeed a pioneering work, geography not
having an honour school at Oxford until 1933. By the
1620 edition there were some nine thousand words on
North America, recounting briefly the arrival of the
Spaniards and the French and Drake's rescue of Ralph
Lane and his company from their plight in Virginia.
He mentions the two companies set up to found
colonies and their failure due to lack of state support. If Abbot's is the only hand in later editions,
there may well be some personal feeling here inasmuch
as Abbot held a £75 share in the Virginia Company under
its third charter of 1612. It might have been in this
connection that Samuel Purchas dedicated Purchas his
pilgrimage to Abbot in the next year, although Purchas'

appointment as Abbot's chaplain soon after may
indicate mere preferment seeking. Abbot was also a
founder member of the North West Passage Company, and
his interests in these ventures were in part due to
the trading activities of his youngest brother,
Morris, later Lord Mayor of London, prominent as a
member of the King's Council for the Virginia Company,
and one of the King's nominees for the company's
treasureship. As a member of the Privy Council, Abbot
found himself at meetings discussing the affairs of
the company, notably after the French complaint of
Samuel Argall's attack on their base at Mount Desert
under the orders of Thomas Dale, the acting Governor.
The Council members were unwilling, however, to commit
themselves until they heard Argall's report to the
Company.

Thus by way of Oxford and court patronage and
after fleeting appointments to the sees of Leicester
and London, Abbot came to the primacy, to hold it for
twenty-two years. Until the rise of William Laud he
had to be noticed, even if at the most critical occa-
sions he failed to get his way.

In comparison with Archbishops Laud and Bancroft,
Abbot has been dealt with scantily even if frequently
by historians. Up to the second half of the last
century the dutiful reference given to Abbot as primate varied in its opinion according to the author's
preconceived theological standpoint. With S.R.
Gardiner and Sir Sidney Lee came an attempt to be impartial, but only lately have such writers as Hugh
Trevor-Roper and Christopher Hill tried to show
Abbot's influence rather than his personality. Not
until the quatercentenary of his birth, October 1962,
did a full-scale biography of Abbot appear, by the
Rev. Dr. P.A. Welsby. Accusations are now made less
against what he believed than against what he did, or
did not, do: his slackness in administration and over
fondness for the life of a courtier in a corrupt
court. In his life of Laud, Trevor-Roper notes that
Abbot "preached Puritan doctrines [but] that did not
matter much: for the danger lay in [their] implica-
tions, which he rejected." In a History today article
[no. 177] he further attacked Abbot as "a skilful
courtier, indifferent, negligent, secular."

Certainly, in his relations with the body of his Church, Abbot was inactive, or at least ineffectual, but from the time of his appointment nothing more was expected from him. James I found him, as Trevor-Roper describes, after his own mind theologically, and, even though he did not believe bishops were anything more than senior administrative ministers, Abbot was not opposed to either episcopacy in particular or the Anglican settlement in general. More than his rival, Lancelot Andrewes, he could be relied upon to keep the Puritans contented and not to stir them up, thus jeopardizing the balance between Church and state: under Abbot there would at least be none of Bancroft's or of Laud's deprivations of Puritans. Inactivity was not mere laziness, it was part of a policy. Its importance was that it gave the already strong Puritans time to consolidate and made them all the more used to going their own ways, although Abbot has been accused by Hill of browbeating the parish clergy, so that when Laud turned the tables the opposition to him was all the greater. Meanwhile, Laud had been baulked since the time when Abbot was criticizing his Oxford theses and had seen Abbot attempting to squash any opinion that could be called Arminian and flirting with continental and Scottish Protestantism. A great force was ready to meet an intransigent new archbishop in 1633, and disaster became inevitable. But although one must admit that Abbot was more fitted to be pro-fessor of divinity at Oxford than Archbishop of Canterbury it is true that, except for his court activities,Abbot reflected more accurately than Laud those who remained in the Church of England before the Civil War.

The lay Puritan mind would not understand Abbot's joining the anti-Howard faction to play politics by introducing Buckingham to the King to be a new favorite, his putting himself in a position to kill Peter Hawkins by going hunting at all, his never being a parish priest. But it required some in-fluence to become Archbishop of Canterbury and to retain one's due place in the nation's affairs if one came only from middle-class stock of a provincial town and was, even if talented enough to become a D.D., not "in the rich flowering of Anglican faith and Worship" (Dr. Higham). Abbot climbed by way of the Earls of

Dorset and Dunbar, and without these the Puritans
would never have had such an amenable archbishop.
But had Abbot had the stroke of genius not to launch
himself lethargically and deeply into theological
waters (a practice not hindered by association with
such a would-be theologian as James I) and so divert
attention to obscure texts from such obviously right
stands as was his in the Essex divorce case, he might
have done a more positive service to the doctrines he
claimed to support.

For reference purposes I give an outline of
Abbot's life, based on the DNB article:

29 Oct. 1562	Born at Guildford.
c. 1570-78	Educated at Guildford Royal Grammar School.
1578-82	Balliol College, Oxford. B.A., 1582.
1583-97	Fellow of Balliol. M.A., 1585; B.D., 1593; D.D., 1597.
1585	Ordained deacon.
1597-1609	Master of University College, Oxford. Vice-chancellor, 1600, 1603, 1605.
6 March 1599/1600	Installed as Dean of Winchester.
1600	Gives judgement on restoration of Cheapside Cross.
1604	Present at Hampton Court Conference and included in a committee to translate the Bible.
1606	Helps to quash Overall's doctrine of nonresistance in Convocation.
1608	Death of Abbot's first patron, the Earl of Dorset.
1608-10	Assists in restoration of episcopal power in Scotland and consecrates bishops in 1610.
27 May 1609	Nominated as Bishop of Lichfield and Coventry.
12 Feb. 1609/10	Enthroned as Bishop of London.

1610	Helps to establish Pembroke College, Oxford.
26 Jan. 1610/11	Chosen to be Archbishop of Canterbury.
1611	Supports powers of High Commission against Coke.
1611/12	Approves the execution of Legate and Wightman.
1612	Participation in North West Passage Company and third Virginia Company.
Oct. 1612	Death of Prince Henry.
1612/13	Opposes ideas of Vorstius and Grotius.
1613	Essex divorce case.
1615	Introduces Villiers (Buckingham) to Court.
1618	Opposes Declaration of Sports and sits at Raleigh's trial.
1619	Founds Hospital of the Blessed Trinity at Guildford.
24 July 1621	Shooting accident, for which he is pardoned by the end of the year.
1623	Opposes Prince Charles's Spanish adventure.
1624	Forbids publication of <u>A gagg for the new Gospel</u>?
27 March 1625	Death of James I. Accession of Charles I.
1627	Refuses to license Sibthorpe's sermon and is sequestered, although restored to favour by the end of 1628.
4 Aug. 1633	Dies at Croydon. Buried at Guildford.

B   SCOPE AND SOURCES OF THE BIBLIOGRAPHY

This bibliography is concerned only with printed books and other writings by and about George Abbot. Many of his letters and valuable materials about him are of an archival nature and remain in MS in the Public Record Office and elsewhere (see Appendix).

PART I is an attempt to record those of Abbot's writings, public and private, which have been printed in full.

Normally where a work of Abbot's appears as part of a larger work I have referred only to the first edition of each such larger work, but where there is a later revised or more accessible edition this is noted.

Part I is divided into seven sections:

A. <u>Works first published in Abbot's lifetime</u>. For separately published works I have given descriptions of all editions I have seen, and this section includes contemporary publication of Abbot's official writings. Earlier lists have appeared in Wood's <u>Athenae Oxonienses</u>, <u>Biographia Britannica</u>, Watt's <u>Bibliotheca Britannica</u>, the <u>Dictionary of national biography</u>, and the <u>Short-title catalogue</u> of Pollard and Redgrave and of Donald Wing; Madan's <u>Oxford books</u> also lists works by and concerning Abbot connected with Oxford. The first four sources named did not give full details of editions of his <u>Geography</u> but did list works published abroad. Several other issues have been noted of works not distinguished by short title alone; also, my entries 4 and 32 have emerged as different from nos. 3 and 29, with which STC equates them. I have tried to inspect the copies of these books in London, Oxford, Cambridge, and Dublin; when none was available in these cities I have relied on information by post from other libraries.

B. <u>Posthumously published works</u>, i.e., the personal accounts of the Essex divorce case, the shooting accident, and the sequestration. For convenience I have also given details of connected letters in this section rather than in the next. Most editions of these accounts are included in collections, and the 56-page separate narrative of the divorce case mentioned in BB remains untraced.

C. <u>Letters</u>. This section does not include summarized or calendared letters, but does attempt to list all published appearances. The note on p. 79

indicates briefly formal commendations which were not
published contemporarily. Sources here are so
scattered that I am far from claiming completeness
for this section.

D. <u>Sermons and speeches</u>. The notes regarding
letters apply here also, although summaries of
sermons are included.

E. <u>Archiepiscopal business</u>. This is concerned
mostly with visitation articles. My main source for
these has been the MS "Index locupletissimus rerum
quae continentur in registro Georgio Abbott" at Lambeth Palace, which lists all visitations made by
Abbot. This I have checked with STC and the British
Museum catalogue for printed editions of the articles
coinciding with the dates given at Lambeth.

When the document is not in Abbot's name,
official business is in Part II, e-f.

F. <u>Abbot's will</u>.

G. <u>Works attributed to Abbot</u>. Works attributed
to Abbot fall into two groups:

1. Those works which later editorial lapses have
    ascribed to Abbot. I have excluded works
    written by other George Abbots when the
    British Museum catalogue ascribes them
    correctly.
2. The speech or letter of 18 July 1623. This
    is dealt with fully in entries 124-35.

PART II is a list of the works about Abbot with
some original importance as well as of some which, if
not original, are among the better-known references to
Abbot and must be considered.

The old histories of the period almost all con-
tain at least a brief "character" of Abbot, and the
most famous or notorious of these have been used with
or without acknowledgement in most later general
works. Several are printed on pages 155-58 of
Welsby's biography. But as encyclopaedia and biographical dictionary references to Abbot as well as
the inevitable panegyrics in local histories and guide-

books are almost entirely derivative, I have omitted
most such references. While I give a few entries on
Abbot's Guildford connections, I have not gone far
into the history of Abbot's Hospital, which itself
holds most of the relevant MS documents.

Since the first submission of this work, Dr.
Welsby's biography, mentioned above, has appeared,
and to its bibliography this part now forms an ex-
pansion, a supplement to the end of 1962, and an
alternative arrangement by subject. I have attempted
to catch the more or less fleeting earlier references
to Abbot and to books such as Robert Sibthorpe's,
with which Abbot was concerned. The section of dedications to Abbot, originally consisting of only
fourteen accidentally discovered entries, now owes
most of its existence to F.B. Williams' Index of
dedications and commendatory verses.

The sources to which I have referred for this
bibliography are listed on pages x-xii. Unless otherwise stated, all works noted are in the British
Museum, an insular limitation which, though incon-
venient for the American reader, is inevitable. For
older work a valuable source is the MS material in
Guildford PL centred on John Russell's edition of the
BB article (no. 157). The hand is mostly that of John
Russell's son Thomas, who seems to have tried to write
a biography supplementing his father's work by copying
every reference, however small, which he could find.
Not all these references are identified, and still
more are omitted from this bibliography as being
entirely derivative.

APPENDIX. Printed calendars and indexes listing
MSS relevant to Abbot are cited. Important holdings
are starred.

C   ARRANGEMENT AND DESCRIPTION OF THE WORKS

PART I. The arrangement and description are de-
gressive because it is not necessary to give a full
description of a letter printed in a nineteenth-
century collection. I am well aware that most of
nos. 1-39 are a contribution to English bibliography

rather than to the study of history, most of these works being theological tracts directed lengthily and turgidly against the Roman Catholic Church.

For contributions to collected works and works in later compilations, the entries follow the lines of Part II.

Full transcriptions are given of titlepages of monograph works and of those titlepages which mention Abbot as an author. Different sizes of capitals are not shown, nor are ligatures or long s; a long s is to be assumed for all initial or medial lower case s's unless otherwise stated. Only in nos. 26 and 26a do these departures from full transcription fail to mark different titlepages, and there a note is given. The Latin combinations ae and oe are always to be taken as diphthongs.

Next come format, collation by signatures and pagination, lines per text page, and running titles. When the running titles vary to indicate chapter headings or subject matter, they are described merely by the word "Contents". Errors in pagination which do not cause the last numbered page to belie the actual number of pages are also shown.

The contents of the book give the first page (by signature) of each section described; matter taken from the book itself is in quotation marks, but capitalization has been adjusted and omissions are indicated. Sources of information, copies seen, and in section A other copies not seen are noted. For a list of libraries used and abbreviations adopted for them, see page ix.

In section A works are arranged in order of the publication of the first edition of each work, followed by later editions. A new number is used for each edition or work given a separate STC or Wing number. Other issues are indicated by letters after the original number.

By issue is meant a work differing from the original only on its titlepage, whether or not the new titlepage is a cancel. By variant, listed in

footnote, is meant differences within the edition or
issue not affecting the titlepage.

Letters, sermons, and speeches are listed chrono-
logically, with headings taken from the original
source if possible.

PART II. The arrangement is largely chrono-
logical, but the criteria for this vary: in section
A (General) and G (Dedications to Abbot) the order
is based upon the date the work was written; in C
(Academic life) and E (Court and politics), upon the
date of the events described; in D (Theology) and F
(Local connections) there is some subject division.
B (Family) is purely alphabetical.

The division between theological and political
aspects cannot be absolutely rigid, but in general
I have placed with theology matters concerning Abbot
and the churches but not interfering with his relations with the Crown and Parliament.

In Part II pre-1800 books are treated slightly
differently from those published later. In all
cases only the first edition of each work is described unless useful editorial matter has been added
later or a reprint made of a scarce work. Modern
practice in capitalization has been followed, but
spelling has been maintained as on the titlepage.
Quotations and the author's name and qualifications
have been omitted without indication. For convenience, descriptions of authors in headings are
given as they appear in the British Museum catalogue.

In pre-1800 books punctuation and all the imprint
are given as on the titlepage, although qualifications
such as "in Pauls Churchyard" are omitted and the imprint date is always in Arabic numerals, preceded by a
comma. Format is based upon bibliographical consider-
ations, but signatures are omitted unless there is no
pagination or it is necessary to refer to unnumbered
pages. Since indexes and some prefaces are not
paginated, every page included in a complete copy is
included in the pagination statement. STC, Wing, and
Madan numbers are given when possible.

For later books punctuation and imprint are in conventional form, and format is given only as a guide to size. The pagination statement includes only the printed pages. Publishers of periodicals are not mentioned. For reprints and analytical entries format is omitted, and only the relevant pages are given.

If the work has been listed before, only a short title is given, followed by a reference to a fuller entry. If no note of a reference to Abbot is made, passim references ascertainable from the index of the work should be understood.

APPENDIX. Only brief titles for purposes of identification are cited. These entries are not indexed.

INDEXES. References are to the number of the item; the first number given is that of the fullest entry. There are three indexes:

A includes all Abbot's works in alphabetical order, works where his name is in the title, and all letters to him.

B includes author and title entries for the whole bibliography except for Abbot as author, but including titles of works by Abbot. Periodicals and books mentioned in notes (n after a reference number) and societies and institutions as publishers of periodicals and as subjects are entered. Authorship of a work is denoted by a colon after the author's name, other connections between person or institution and work are shown by a hyphen, passing references by a comma. Biographies, diaries, and letters are entered only under the person concerned unless they have a distinctive title. Articles are omitted from all titles. In the index the original spelling of titles has been retained, but alphabetical order is governed by the modern spelling. I and J, U and V, are written according to present-day usage.

Entries are made under all forms of names if there are only one or two entries; otherwise a reference is made to one acceptable form. As an ex-

ception, all bishops are entered under their surnames
with references from all their sees, since a
specific entry at YORK, <u>Archbishop</u>, for the letter
Harsnet received while still at Norwich would be un-
necessary and misleading. References to Archbishop
Abbot are simply to "Abbot"; his relations are given
initials.

    C is an index of identified pre-1700 printers
and booksellers for separately published works in
Part I, A.

PART I

WORKS BY GEORGE ABBOT

1   <u>1598</u>   <u>Q</u>UAESTIONES <u>SEX</u>

QVAESTIO- / NES SEX, TOTI- / DEM PRAELECTIO- /
NIBVS, IN SCHOLA / THEOLOGICA, OXONIAE, /
PRO FORMA, HABITIS, / DISCVSSAE, ET /
DISCEPTATAE. / ANNO. 1597. / IN QVIBVS, E
SACRA SCRIP- / TVRA, ET PATRIBVS AN- /
tiquissimis, quid statuendum / sit, definitur:
/ PER GEORGIVM ABBATEM / tunc Collegij
Baliolensis / socium. / Johan. 9.4 <u>Venit nox</u>
<u>quum nemo potest operari</u>. / Gregor. Nazianz.
Orat. 21. <u>Vtinam ex eorum sim</u> / <u>numero, qui</u>
<u>pro veritate decertant, & in homi-</u> / <u>num</u>
<u>offensionem incurrent</u>. / [type orns.] /
OXONIAE, / Ex Officinâ JOSEPHI BARNESII Typo-
/ graphicâ. M.D. XCVIII.

4°. ¶|⁴, ¶|¶|², A-Z⁴, Aa-Ff⁴. pp.[12], 1-21,
[1], 23-24, 35-224, [18]. = 244. 32 lines.
r.t. Contents.
Errors: Ff missigned F. p. 82 misnumbered 68.

    1a, [type orns.] / [A] / [type orns.] :
¶|1b, blank: ¶|2a, t.p.: ¶|2b, blank: ¶|3a,
"Honoratissimo viro, B. Thomae Sackvillo,
Baroni Buckhurstio ... S." [preface dated
University College Oxford 16 May 1598.]:
¶| ¶| 2a, "Hoc opere continentur, <u>etc</u>.": C3b,
blank: C4a, text, beginning with chapter
heading of the first question: Dd4a, "Index
rerum praecipuarum quae in hoc opere
continentur.": Ff3b, 4a, 4b, blank.

STC 36   Madan i. 1598/1.

Seen: LLP LW C DT O.   Not seen: CE DC
    DU EU Newcastle C Norwich PL.

These theses were presented by Abbot in 1597
for the degree of Doctor of Divinity in the
University of Oxford. The titles of the theses

are recorded on the titlepage of the 1616
edition (no. 2) and are here presented in
the same order.

DT wants ¶1 and Ff^4.

1616 edition

2   GEORGII ABBATTI / REVERENDISSIMI / ARCHIEPISCOPI
    / CANTVARIENSIS / Explicatio sex illustrium
    Quaestionum, / I. De Mendacio. / II. De
    Circumcisione & Baptismo. / III. De Astrologia.
    / IV. De praesentia in cultu Idololatrico. /
    V. De fuga in persequutione & peste. / VI. An
    Deus sit author peccati? / Oxoniae anno 1597.
    in schola Theologica proposita, ibidem edita:
    / & nunc primum in Germania recusa. /[device:
    in a rectangle, an oval flanked by cherubs,
    within the oval Jonah being cast ashore, and
    the inscription "Fata viam invenient" around
    the oval] / FRANCOFVRTI. Prostat apud IONAM
    ROSAM. / [half rule] / M.DC.XVI.   [stet
    Idololatrico.]

    4°. *^{4}, A-Y^4, Z^2, Aa^2. pp. [8], 1-174, [10].
       = 192. 33 lines. r.t. Contents.
       Errors: p. 163 misnumbered 193. r.t. Q2a
           "Caput Quintum" instead of "Caput
           Quartum".

    *1a, t.p.: *1b, blank: *2a, "Cl.V.M.Martino
    Füsselio Serenissimo electori Brandenburgico ...
    Abrahamus Scultetus. S.D.": *4b, blank: A1a,
    "Christiano lectori.": C1b, text, beginning
    with chapter heading of the first question:
    Y4a-Aa2b, "Index rerum, etc."

    DGK p. 66.

    Seen: LW   C   DM   DN   DT   O.

    The printer is Abraham Scultetus.

    LW has the signature of John Donne on the title-
    page and a blank leaf before the titlepage with
    its stub between *4 and A1a,

1599.   A BRIEF DESCRIPTION OF THE WHOLE WORLD

3 A / BRIEFE DESCRIP- / TION OF THE / whole worlde.
/ WHEREIN IS PARTI- / cularly described, all the
Monarchies, / Empires, and kingdomes of the same:
/ with their seuerall titles and / scituations
thereunto / adioyning. / [woodcut: rose and
flowers] / AT LONDON / Printed by T. Iudson,
for Iohn Browne, / and are to be sould at the
signe of the / Bible in Fleete-streete. / 1599.

4°. A-D^{8}, E^{2}. No pagination or foliation.   68
   pages. 34 lines. r.t. Contents.

Ala, t.p.: Alb, blank: A2a, text: E2b, blank.

STC 24.

Seen: L(2 copies) DU(c.e.).

Latin chapter headings and running titles.

L (Harley 6533) is an interleaved edition, lack-
ing the titlepage. A typed note is inserted as
follows: "The notes and additions in Harl. 6533
bring the 1st. ed. roughly (not exactly) into
line with the 5th ed., but the latter has some
additional matter, notably the last section on
'Those Countries that lie about the two Poles'.
Possibly this ed. (Harl. 6533) corresponds with
the 3rd. or 4th editions". In fact, 51 leaves
are inserted as required, and the additions and
corrections do not bring the text up to that of
either the "third Edition" of 1608 or even that
of the 1605 imprint (not in L; see no. 6).
There seems, however, no reason why anyone
should have made these additions save under
Abbot's auspices or those of another reviser
who may have taken over the work. The catalogue
of the Harleian MSS says that the notes are by
Jo: Davies, to whom the book belonged.

Book-auction records now enters this work and
its subsequent editions under Botero, claiming
that Abbot and Robert Johnson translated it
from G. Botero's Relationi universali (Ferrara,

1592), which Johnson alone translated into
English as The travellers breviat (London,
1601 and later editions). This work might well
have been taken as a model by Abbot, since the
contents are arranged in practically the same
order, starting with Spain and placing the
British Isles with the islands in pt. 6, but
it is a far longer work of (probably) 562
pages. The first edition of Johnson's translation is again a briefer work than the
original and is put into a different order;
there is no ascription to Botero in it, and
the translation is very free; it too might
only have been inspired by Botero. All three
works are described in E. G. R. Taylor's Late
Tudor and early Stuart geography (London, 1934).

According to the DNB, Abbot wrote his Geography,
as it came to be known, for the instruction of
his pupils when he was Master of University
College, Oxford. H. Savage in Balliofergus
claims that P. Heylin took Abbot's Geography
as a model for his Microcosmus (1621 and later
editions); it does indeed retain the arrangement of topics of Abbot's and Botero's works.

"A brieff description of sea and land" was
entered in the Stationers' Register to John
Browne on 24 May 1599 (Arber v. 3, p. 145).

1599, new edition

4   A / BRIEFE DESCRIP- / TION OF THE / whole
    worlde. / WHEREIN ARE PAR- / ticularly
    described all the Monarchies, / Empires, and
    kingdomes of the same: / with their seuerall
    titles and / situations thereunto / adioyning.
    [woodcut: rose and flowers] / AT LONDON /
    Printed by T. Iudson, for Iohn Browne, / and
    are to be sould at the signe of the / Bible
    in Fleete-streete. / 1599.

    4°. A-H^4. No pagination or foliation. 64 pages.
       35 lines. r.t. Contents.

Ala, t.p.: Alb, blank: A2a, text: H4b, blank.

STC 24 - another edition.

Seen: CE.

Latin chapter headings and running titles.

The text is the same as that of the first edition, with orthographical differences only.

CE is from Archbishop Sancroft's library.

1600 edition

5   A / BRIEFE / DESCRIP- / TION OF THE / whole worlde. / WHEREIN ARE PAR- / ticularly described al the Monarchies, / Empires, and kingdomes of the same: / with their seuerall titles and / situations therevnto / adioyning. / [woodblock: a rectangle, man's head breathing fire, flanked by foliage] / AT LONDON / Printed by R.B. for Iohn Browne, / and are to be sould at thesigne of the / Bible inFleet-streete. / 1600. [stet thesigne inFleet]

4°. A-H^4. No pagination or foliation. 64 pages. 35 lines. r.t. Contents.

Ala, t.p.: Alb, blank: A2a, text: H4b, blank.

STC 25.

Seen: L O WF(c.e.).

Text the same as no. 4, but type ornaments on A2a different and caption title has "World", while both 1599 printings have "Worlde". A page-for-page reprint.

The printer is Richard Braddock.

<u>1605, enlarged edition</u>

6   A / Briefe Description / of the whole / WORLDE.
    / Wherein is particularly described all the
    Mo- / narchies, Empires, and Kingdomes of the
    / same: newly augmented and enlar- / ged: with
    their seuerall titles / and scituations
    thereunto / adioyning / [device: McK.188b] /
    AT LONDON / Printed for Iohn Browne, and are
    to be / sold at his Shoppe in S. <u>Dunstans</u> /
    Churchyard in Fleet-streete, / 1605.

    4°. A-V^4, X^2. No pagination or foliation.
        84 pages. 35 lines. r.t. Contents.
        Errors: H3 not signed.

    A1a, t.p.: A1b, blank: A2a, text: X1b, end of
    text, "Finis", woodcut the same as that on the
    titlepage of the <u>Treatise</u> of 1624 (no. 25):
    X2a-b, "Vniuersities" [excludes Oxford and
    Cambridge].

    STC 26.

    Seen: C   CH(m.f. at O).

    The text is considerably expanded, even beyond
    that of the MS additions to the interleaved
    copy (L: Harley 6533). The section on Spain
    is extended from 13 lines to more than 3 pages;
    there is an outburst against religious houses
    in England; and for the first time there is a
    chapter on the Arctic and Antarctic regions.
    Latin chapter headings and running titles.

    The printer is William White, who held the
    woodcut on X1b in 1613 (Sayle 2312) and the
    device 1600-14 (see McK. 188) before passing
    them to Milbourne (see no. 25) and Matthewes
    respectively.

1608, "third Edition"

7 A / Briefe Description / of the whole / Worlde
/ Wherein is particularly described all the /
Monarchies, Empires and Kingdomes of / the
same, with their Academies. / Newly augmented
and enlarged; / with their seuerall titles
and / scituations thereunto / adioyning. /
The third Edition. / [woodcut: head on U-shaped
strapwork, flanked by branches] / At London /
Printed for Iohn Browne, and are to be / sold
at his shoppe in Saint Dunstans / Churchyard in
Fleetstreet. / 1608.

4°. A-V^4. No pagination or foliation. 80 pages.
35 lines. r.t. Contents.
Errors: F3 not signed. I3 missigned J3.

Ala, t.p.: Alb, blank: A2a, text: V4a-b,
"Vniversities".

STC 27.

Seen: L LLP O WF(c.e).   Not seen: Peterborough C.

The text is the same as the 1605 edition, but
there are English chapter headings and running
titles and it is not a page-for-page reprint.

The printer is Richard Braddock (note in WF
catalogue).

LLP copy is from Archbishop Bancroft's library.

1617, "fourth Edition"

8 A / Briefe Description / of the whole / VVorld.
/ VVherein is particularly described all the /
Monarchies, Empires and Kingdomes of / the
same, with their Academies. / Newly augmented
and enlarged; / with their seuerall Titles and
/ scituations thereunto / adioyning / [rule] /
The fourth Edition. / [rule] / [woodcut: as in

no. 7] / At London / Printed for <u>Iohn Browne</u>,
and are to be / sold at his Shoppe in <u>Saint</u>
<u>Dunstans</u> / Churchyard in Fleet-streete. / 1617.
[Dunstans, st is ligature with short s]

4°. A-Y^4. No pagination or foliation. 176 pages.
    35 lines. r.t. Contents.
    Errors: L3 not signed. L2 missigned K2. c.w.
      L2a "least", first word L2b "lest" (both
      should be "lest").

A1a, blank except for "A": A1b, blank: A2a,
t.p.: A2b, blank: A3a, text: Y4a-b,
"Vniuersities".

STC 28.

Seen: L CE CH(m.f. at O) CT WF(c.e.).
    Not seen: EU.

The text has been expanded for the first time
since 1605, e.g. there are now five pages on
Spain. Twenty lines occupy 35/16".

The printer is Thomas Snodham (note in WF
    catalogue).

A1 is missing from L and CE.

<u>Variant</u>
CE: c.w. L2a "least", first word L2b "least".

<u>1620, "fift Edition"</u>

9 A Briefe Description / of the whole / VVorld.
  / VVherein is particularly described all the /
  Monarchies, Empires and Kingdomes of / <u>the</u>
  <u>same, with their Academies</u>. / Newly augmented
  and enlarged; / with their seuerall Titles
  and / scituations thereunto / adioyning/
  [rule] / <u>The fift Edition</u>. / [rule] /
  [woodcut: as in no. 7] / At London / Printed
  for <u>Iohn Marriot</u>, and are to be / sold at his
  Shop in <u>Saint Dunstons</u> Church- / yard in
  Fleet-street, 1620.

4°. A-Y^4. No pagination or foliation. 176 pages.
   35 lines. r.t. Contents.
   Errors: L3 not signed. r.t. Fla "Of
       Greec, &c."

Ala, blank [see also below]: Alb, blank:
A2a, t.p.: A2b, blank: A3a, text: Y4a-b,
"Vniuersities."

STC 29.

Seen: L LU C CH(m.f. at O) WF(c.e.).
   Not seen: Dulwich College.

A line-for-line reprint of the 1617 edition,
but mistakes on L2 have been corrected and some
type founts changed. Twenty lines occupy
$3^3/16$".

The printer is Thomas Snodham (note in Sayle).

Variant
C: Ala has "A" on it.

1624, "sixt Edition"

10 A Briefe Description / of the whole / World. /
    [rule] / Wherein is particularly described, /
    all the Monarchies, Empires, and / Kingdomes
    of the same, with their / ACADEMIES. / [rule]
    / Newly augmented and enlarged, with / their
    seuerall Titles and Scituations / thereunto
    adioyning. / [rule] / The sixt Edition. /
    [rule] / [type ornaments] / [rule] / LONDON, /
    Printed for IOHN MARRIOT, and are to bee /
    sold at his Shop in Saint Dunstons Church- /
    yard in Fleet-street. 1624.

4°. A-Y^4. No pagination or foliation. 176 pages.
   36 lines. r.t. Contents.
   Errors: H3 not signed.

Ala, probably blank: Alb, probably blank:
A2a, t.p.: A2b, blank: A3a, text: Y4a-b:
"Vniuersities".

STC 30.

Seen: L WF(c.e.).   Not seen: Lincoln C.

A sheet-for-sheet reprint of the 1620 edition,
with marginal notes for the first time and 1/3
column "Of England" after the "Universities"
section giving the numbers of counties,
dioceses, etc.

Mrs. Browne passed the stocks and publishing
rights of this work to Marriot on 17 Feb.
1622/23 (Arber v. 4, p. 92).

The printer is Augustine Mathewes (note in WF
    catalogue).

L lacks A1.

1634, new edition

11   [Within a double rule] A BRIEFE / DESCRIPTION
      / OF THE WHOLE / WORLD. / Wherin is
      particularly descri- / bed all the Monarchies,
      Empires / and Kingdomes of the same, with /
      their ACADEMIES. / As also their severall
      Titles / and Situations thereunto / adjoyning.
      / [rule] / Written by the Right Reverend /
      Father in God, George, late Arch- / Bishop
      of Canterburie. / [rule] / [type orns.] /
      [rule] / LONDON, / Printed for William Sheares,
      at the / signe of the Harrow in Bri- / taines
      Bursse. 1634.

      12°. A-O^{12}. pp. [4], 1-329, [3]. = 336.
          29 lines. r.t. Contents.
          Errors: pp. misnumbered - 184 for 148,
              209-10 for 210-11, 112 for 212,
              259 for 260. r.t. p. 301 "Of Peru
              ann Brasile."

Engraved titlepage inserted after A1; described
in Johnson p. 38 (Marshall 16) and illustrated.
Foot reads: Printed for Will: Sheares, at the
Harrow in Britaines burse. / 1634.

Ala-b, blank: engraved t.p. follows: A2a, t.p.:
A2b, blank: A3a, text: O1la, "Vniversities":
O12b, "Of England."

STC 31.

Seen: C CH(m.f. at O) GuA O LC(c.e.)
    WF(c.e.).

Now that Abbot was dead, this work appeared
with his name as author. The text has again
been expanded.

The printer is Thomas Harper (note in WF
    catalogue).

GuA lacks engraved t.p. WF and O lack Al.

1635, new edition

x12 [Within a double rule] A BRIEFE / DESCRIPTION /
OF THE WHOLE / WORLD, / Wherein is particularly
descri- / bed all the Monarchies, Empires / and
Kingdomes of the same, with / their ACADEMIES.
/ As also their severall Titles / and Situations
thereunto / ajoyning. / [rule] / Written by the
Right Reverend / Father in God, George, late
Arch- / bishop of Canterburie. / [rule] / [type
orns.] / LONDON / Printed for William Sheares,
at the / signe of the Harrow in Bri- / taines
Bursse. 1635.

12°. A-P^{12}. pp. [5], 2-350, [6]. = 360.
    28 lines. r.t. Contents. [The collation
    assumes Al was not deliberately excised.]
    Errors: not reported.

Engraved titlepage inserted before A2, as in
no. 11. Dated 1634.

Ala-b, missing, probably blank: engraved t.p.
follows: A2a, t.p.: A2b, blank: A3a, text:
P12b, blank. [The location of the "Universities"
section was not reported.]

Ramage   STC 31after.

Information by letter from DU and LC(c.e.);
L (has t.p. only in Ames collection of frag-
ments, v. 2, pt. 2, no. 1291).

DU and LC copies lack A1, DU lacks engraved t.p.

1636, new edition

13   [Within a single rule at head and foot, double
     rules at sides] A BRIEFE / DESCRIPTION / OF THE
     WHOLE / WORLD. / Wherein is particularly
     described / all the Monarchies, Empires, and /
     Kingdomes of the same, with / their ACADEMIES.
     / As also their severall Titles and /
     Situations thereunto / adjoyning. / Written by
     the Most Reverend / Father in God, GEORGE, /
     late Arch-bishop of / Canterbury. / [rule] /
     LONDON, / Printed by T.H. for Will. Sheares,
     and / are to be sold at the signe of the
     Harrow / in Brittains Burse. 1636.

     12°. A-P^{12}. pp. [5], 2-350, [6] = 360.
        28 lines. r.t. Contents. [The collation
        assumes that A1 was not deliberately
        excised.]
        Error: r.t. p. 343 "the two Poles" for
           "neere the two Poles."

     Engraved titlepage inserted (mounted) before
     A2, as in no. 11, but foot reads: Printed for
     Will: Sheares at the Bible in Couen Garden.
     [1642 is added in MS in L.]

     A1a-b, missing, probably blank: engraved t.p.:
     A2a, t.p.: A2b, blank: A3a, text: P9b,
     "Universities": P12b, "Of England".

     STC 32.

     Seen: L.

     The text is unchanged from 1634 except for
     orthographical variations. Since the 1635

edition was not inspected, I cannot say whether
this is a new edition or merely a reissue.

The printer is Thomas Harper (note in WF
   catalogue).

The Bibliographical Society's relevant <u>Handlist
of Printers</u> does not credit a shop in Covent
Garden to Sheares until 1642, so the e.t.p. is
probably inserted from a later edition.

Another issue

13a   [As no. 13 to] / <u>LONDON</u>, / Printed by <u>T.H.</u> and are
       to be sold by / <u>Wil. Sheares</u> at the signe of
       the Harrow / in <u>Brittains</u> Burse. 1636.

In all other respects similar to no. 13.

STC 32 - another issue.

Seen: O   WF(c.e.).

Both O and WF lack A1; O lacks the engraved
titlepage.

1642, new edition

14   [Within a border of type orns.]   A BRIEFE /
      DESCRIPTION / <u>OF THE WHOLE</u> / WORLD. / VVherein
      is particularly de- / scribed all the
      Monarchies, Empires / and Kingdomes of the
      same, with their / ACADEMIES. / As also their
      severall Titles and Situations thereunto
      adjoyning. / [seven short rules] / Written by
      the most Reverend / Father in God, <u>GEORGE</u>,
      late / Arch-bishop of <u>Canterbuy</u> / [seven short
      rules] / <u>LONDON</u>. / Printed by <u>B. Alsop</u>, and
      are to be sold by / <u>VVilliam Sheares</u>, at the
      signe of the Harrow in <u>Brittaines</u> Burse. [stet
      Canterbuy.]

      12°: A-O^{12}. pp. [4], 1-329, [3]. = 336.
          29 lines. r.t. Contents. [The collation

     assumes that A1 was not deliberately
     excised.]
     Errors: pp. misnumbered - 11 for 18, 43 for
        42, 42 for 43, 75 for 57, 96 for 94,
        149 for 146, 122 for 212, 280 for 260,
        222 for 322, 224 for 324. D3 missigned
        D4, E4 missigned A4, G5 unsigned, O2
        missigned G2. pp. 1, 22, 24, "43", 68
        numbered on inner margin. p. 7 not
        numbered.

A1a-b, missing, probably blank: A2a, t.p.:
A2b, blank: A3a, text: O11a-12b, "Universities."

Wing A60.

Seen: DT.   Not seen: EU (may be 14a).

The copy seen lacks A1. The text is unchanged
from that of 1636.

<u>Book-auction records</u> ascribes an additional
engraved titlepage.

<u>Another issue</u>

14a [As no. 14 to] / <u>LONDON</u>. / Printed by <u>B. Alsop</u>,
    for J.M. and are to be sold by W. Sheares at
    his shop in Coven- / garden, neare the new
    Exchange, 1642.

    Format, collation, pagination, errors, and
    contents as no. 14.

    Wing A60 - another issue.

    Seen: CT.

    The bookseller J.M. is John Marriot.

    The copy seen lacks A1. The 2 in the date
    appears to be printed over a 1.

1656 edition

x15   [Within a border of type orns.]   A BRIEFE /
DESCRIPTION / OF THE WHOLE / WORLD. / WHEREIN
/ Is particularly described / all the
monarchies, empires / and kingdoms of the same,
with / their Academies. / AS ALSO, / Their
severall Titles and Scituati- / ons thereunto
adjoyning. / [rule] / Written by the most
Reverend Fa- / ther in God, George Abbot, late
/ Archbishop of Canterbury. / [rule] / LONDON,
/ Printed for W. Sheares, at the Blew / Bible
in Bedford Street in Coven / Garden, 1656.

12°. A-H^{12}, *^{4}, I-O^{12}. pp. [4], 1-196, 189-329,
[3]. = 344. 27-28 lines. r.t. Contents.
[The collation assumes that A1 was not
deliberately excised.]
Errors: pp. 209 misnumbered 29, 234-35
misnumbered 233-34. r.t. on p. 96 reads
"Of Hungarie and Austria" instead of "Of
Cathaie and China".

Engraved titlepage inserted before A2 as
in no. 13.

A1a-b, missing, probably blank: engraved t.p.:
A2a, t.p.: A2b, blank: A3a text: O11a,
"Universities": O12b, "Of England".

Wing A61.

Seen: CU(c.e.) Y(c.e.).

The printing was divided between two
compositors, or groups of compositors, one
taking $\emptyset$a-I4b and the other $\emptyset$I5a-P of the
1636 edition. They must have been instructed
to save space, and the compositor of the
second part succeeded in doing so in $\emptyset$I-O.
Meanwhile the compositor of the first part was
trying to keep line for line to his copy. This
meant that by the end of his allotted space he
had not saved any pages and on p. 188 (H12b)
the catchword is "their" as in 1636. He thus
had to set $\emptyset$* and duplicate the pagination to
reach the point at which the new $\emptyset$I begins.

Y wants all after p. 190.

1664, "fifth eddition"

16   [Within a double rule] A BRIEFE / DESCRIPTION /
     OF THE WHOLE / WORLD. / WHEREIN / Is
     particularly described / all the Monarchies,
     Empires / and Kingdoms of the same, with /
     their Academies. / As ALSO, / Their severall
     Titles and Scituati- / ons thereunto
     adjoyning. / [rule] / Written by the Reverend
     Father in God / George Abbot, late Archbishop
     of Canterbury. / [rule] / The Fifth Eddition.
     [rule] / LONDON, / Printed for Margaret
     Sheares, at the / Blew Bible in Bedford-Street
     in Coven Garden, / and John Playfere at the
     White-Beare in / the upper Walk in the New
     Exchange. / 1664.

     12°. A-O^{12}, P^4. pp. [4], 1-340. = 344.
       27-28 lines. r.t. Contents.
       Errors: L2 and O5 unsigned. L4 missigned
         L2. pp. 325-32 misnumbered 335-341, 341.
         r.t. - pp. "341", "341": "Of Peru and
         Brasile" instead of "Of the Countries
         near the two Poles", p. 96: "Of
         Hungaria and Austria" instead of "Of
         Cathaie and China", pp. 243-48: "Of
         the islands in the Indian Sea" for "Of
         the islands in the Atlantick Sea".

     A1a-b, blank: A2a, t.p.: A2b, blank: A3a,
     text: P3b, "Universities": P4b [foot], "Of
     England.

     Wing A62.

     Seen: L O.   Not seen: L-Victoria and Albert
        Museum.

     Practically a line-for-line reprint of the 1656
     edition, with the ß* and duplicate pagination
     corrected. "Of Cathaie and China" spreads to
     the top of p. 97, instead of ending at the foot
     of p. 96, and there are similar slight varia-
     tions towards the end of the book.

The pages of the text are within a ruled border.

1599.   VERSES TO JOHN CASE

17 In magnum Academiae lumen J. Casum Georgius Abbas S. Theologiae Doctor.

Appears in:

> CASE, John, M.D., Fellow of St. John's College, Oxford
> Lapsis philosophicus seu commentarius in 8 lib phys: Aristot in quo arcana physiologiae examinantur. Oxoniensi, excudebat Joseph' Barnes' Oxoniae. [1599.] $9¶¶7. STC 4756; Madan i. 1599/2.

The sixth of a series of verses prefacing the work. Abbot's six-line poem begins "Multa tibi natura dedit doctissime Case."

The poem remains in the reissue of 1612 (STC 4757).

1600   AN EXPOSITION UPON THE PROPHET JONAH

18 AN / EXPOSITION / VPON THE PRO- / PHET IONAH. / Contained in certaine Sermons, preached / in S. Maries Church in Oxford. / By GEORGE ABBOT Professor of Diuinitie, / and Maister of Vniuersitie Colledge. / IOHAN. 9.4. / The night cometh when no man can worke. / [device: McK. 192] / LONDON, / Imprinted by Richard Field dwelling in / the Blacke-friers. / 1600.

$4°$. A^4, $B-Z^8$, $Aa-Ss^8$. pp. [8], 1-638, [2].
   37 lines. r.t. Contents.
   Errors: pp. misnumbered - 171 for 183, 104
      for 204, 116 for 216, 132 for 332, 291
      for 335, 373 for 573.

Ala-b, blank: A2a, t.p.: A2b, blank: A3a, "To the Right Honorable my very especiall good

Lord, Thomas Baron of Buckhurst, <u>etc</u>.": B1a,
text [of 30 lectures each beginning "The
chiefe points in the <u>x</u> lecture" and having
the relevant text of <u>J</u>onah]: Ss6b, "To the
reader": Ss8a-b, blank.

STC 34.

Seen: L   C   DM   Not seen: Peterborough C
    St. Andrews U.

In this edition each lecture is headed by a
woodblock and most start on a new page. The
whole text of the Book of Jonah is employed
in the sermons, which were preached between
1594 and 1599.

Entered in the Register 22 Feb. 1599/1600
(Arber v. 3, p. 156).

<u>Another issue</u>

18a [As no. 18 to] / <u>LONDON</u>, / Imprinted by Richard
    Field, and are to be / sold by Richard Garbrand.
    / 1600.

In all other respects similar to no. 18.

STC 34 - another issue.

Seen: LLP   O.

LLP lacks Ss8.

<u>1613, new edition</u>

19 AN / EXPOSITION / VPON THE PRO- / PHET IONAH: /
    <u>Contained in certaine Sermons, preached</u> / in S.
    <u>Maries Church in Oxford</u>: / By GEORGE ABBOT
    Professor of Diuinitie, / and Maister of
    Vniuersitie Colledge. / IOHN. 9.4. / <u>The night</u>
    <u>cometh when no man can worke</u>. / [device: McK.
    192] / LONDON, / Imprinted by Richard Field, /
    1613.

4°. A^4, $B-Z^8$, $Aa-Qq^8$, Rr^2. pp. [6], 1-612, [2].
38 lines. r.t. Contents.
Errors: [see also below]. Pages misnumbered
- 401 for 410, 459 for 439, 533 for 553.

Ala, t.p.: Alb, blank: A2a, "To the Right
Honorable my very especiall good Lord, Thomas
Baron of Buckhurst, etc.": A4a, text [as no.
18]: Rr2a-b, "To the reader".

STC 35.

Seen: L LLP LW C DT GuA.   Not seen:
    Aberdeen U Carlisle C Lincoln C
    Manchester Chethams Newcastle C Norwich PL.

In this edition each lecture is headed by type
ornaments and follows on from the one before
without starting a new page.

Variants
i) C and DT have also pp. 296-97 misnumbered
    288-89, pp. 300-01 misnumbered 292-93.
ii) LLP has 439 correctly numbered; otherwise
    as C.
DT lacks A2-3.

1845, "new edition"

20 AN / EXPOSITION / UPON THE / PROPHET JONAH. /
    BY GEORGE ABBOT, D.D. / ARCHBISHOP OF CANTERBURY.
    / A New Edition, / BY / GRACE WEBSTER: / TO WHICH
    IS ADDED, A LIFE OF THE AUTHOR. / IN TWO VOLUMES.
    / VOL. I. [or, VOL. II.] / LONDON: HAMILTON,
    ADAMS, & CO. / EDINBURGH: CHAS. SMITH, PRINCE'S
    STREET. / MDCCCXLV.

    12°. Vol. 1: π^1, $2\pi^2$, a^6, b^4, $\underline{b}^2$, $A-Z^6$, $Aa-Ee^6$,
    Ff^4. pp. [5], iv, [1], vi-xxiv, [1], yi-viii,
    [1], 2-344. 37 lines. Vol. 2: π^1, $2\pi^2$,
    $A-Z^6$, $Aa-Ff^6$, Gg^2. pp. [5], iv, [1], 2-351,
    [1]. 37 lines. [In vol. 1 the seventh page
    is signed a, p. ix is signed $\underline{b}2$ (possibly
    instead of a2). p. xvii is signed b, the
    page after p. xxiv is signed $\underline{b}$.] r.t.
    Contents.

I. ¶1a, "An exposition upon the prophet Jonah":
   ¶1b, blank: 2¶1a, t.p.: 2¶1 b, "Printed by
   Robert Hardie and company, Frederick Street,
   Edinburgh.":2¶2a, "Contents.": a1a, "The
   life of George Abbot, D.D. Archbishop of
   Canterbury.": b1a, "Epistle dedicatory.":
   A1a, text: Ff4b̄, "End of Vol. I.", imprint
   as on 2¶1b.

II. ¶1a, "An exposition upon the prophet Jonah":
    ¶1b, blank: 2¶1a, t.p.: 2¶1b, "Printed by
    Robert Hardie, etc.": 2¶2a, "Contents": A1a,
    text: Gg1a, "To the reader.": Gg2a, "The
    end", imprint as on 2¶1b: Gg2b, blank.

DNB.

Seen: L DT.

The spelling and punctuation have been modern-
ized; most of the marginal notes have been
removed and some inserted in the text. The
running titles form a commentary on the text.

The introduction gives a list of Abbot's works
and prints the text of Abbot's letter to Naun-
ton (no. 71) and the spurious letter (as no.
132) on pp. xvi-xix.

P. iv has a note "In some of the copies, the
'son of Jonah' is printed by mistake for 'the
son of Joash' in the 6th line of the 3^d page".
L and DT copies have this misprint.

Original casings are maroon cloth with blind
pattern on front and back boards. Spine divided
into four panels by blind-stamped bars. Top
panel lettered: JONAH/ BY / ARCHB^p. ABBOT / VOL.
I [or, II] Bottom panel lettered: WEBSTER'S /
EDITION

<u>1603</u>   VERSES ON THE DEATH OF ELIZABETH I

21 Quae mihi sufficiunt lachrymae, quae flumina
    flenti, Defleo dum cineres Elisabetha tuos?

Appears in:

OXFORD. **University of Oxford**
Oxoniensis academiae funebre officium in
memoriam honoratissimam serenissimae et
beatissimae Elisabethae, nuper Angliae
Franciae, & Hiberniae Reginae. Oxoniae,
excudebat **Iosephus** Barnesius, Almae Academiae Typographus. 1603. pp. 6-7. STC 19018;
Madan i. 1603/9 and ii. 228.

The sixth of a series of poems written by
senior members of the University lamenting
the death of Elizabeth I. Abbot's 30-line
poem begins:

"Quae fuit Henrici ter-maxima filia Magni ..."
It is signed:

"Georgius Abbots Sacr. Theol. Doctor, Magister
Collegij Universitatis, Oxon."

1603   VERSES ON THE ACCESSION OF JAMES I

22 [No heading]

Appears in:

OXFORD. **University of Oxford**
Academiae Oxoniensis pietas erga serenis-
simum et potentissimum Iacobum Anglicae
Scotiae Franciae & Hiberniae Regem, fidei
defensorem, Beatissimae Elisabethae nuper
Reginae legitimè & auspicatissimè succe-
dentem. Oxoniae Excudebat Iosephus
Barnesius, Almae Academiae Typographus.
1603. pp. 10-11. STC 19019; Madan i.
1603/7 and ii. 230.

The eleventh of a series of poems extolling
James I. Abbot's 20-line poem begins:

"Quae fuit Europae lectissima foemina,
princeps ..." It is signed:

"Georgius Abbats, sacrae Theologiae Doct.
Decanus Wintoniensis, Coll. Vniversitatis
Magister."

<u>1604   THE REASONS WHICH DOCTOUR HILL HATH
BROUGHT FOR THE UPHOLDING OF PAPISTRY ...
UNMASKED</u>

23   THE / REASONS / VVHICH DOCTOVR HILL / HATH
BROVGHT, FOR THE / vpholding of Papistry,
which is false=/<u>lie termed the Catholike
Religion: / Vnmasked, and shewed to be very
weake, and vpon exa=/mination most
insufficient for that purpose:</u> / By GEORGE
ABBOT Doctor of Divinity & Deane / <u>of the
Cathedrall Church in VVinchester.</u> / The first
Part. / Joh. 9.4. The night commeth when no man
can worke. / Jer. <u>51.6. Flee out of the
middes of Babylon, and deliver e-/very man
his soule: bee not destroyed in her
ini-/quitie.</u> / [type orns.] / <u>AT OXFORD,</u>
/ Printed by JOSEPH BARNES, & are to be
sold in Paules / Church-yarde at the signe
of the Crowne by / <u>Simon VVaterson.</u> 1604.

4°. ¶^{4}, A-Z^8, Aa-Dd^8, Ee^2, Ff^4. pp. [8],
1-383, 386-438, [8] = 452. 37 lines. r.t.
Contents.
Errors: pp. 125 misnumbered 97, 313 misnumbered 331.

¶1a, McK. 285 with type orns. above and below:
¶1b, blank:¶2a, t.p.:¶2b, blank:¶3a, "Tc the
Right Honorable Thomas Baron of Buckhurst,
etc.":¶4b, blank: A1a, "To D. Hill, as a
briefe answere to his two letters prefixed
before his book.": A5a, text [10 chapters
headed "An answere to the x reason."]: Ff1a,
"To the Christian reader.": Ff4a-b, blank.

STC 37   Madan i. 1604/1 [Madan does not show
italics for "of the Cathedrall"].

Seen: L LLP LW C DT O WF(c.e.).   Not
seen: CE DU Worcester C.

An answer to Hill's <u>A quartron of reasons of catholike religion</u> (no. 232). Only the first part of Abbot's reply was published. From his epilogue it appears that his health had not permitted him to answer the other fifteen reasons. At each stage in the argument Hill's text is prefixed to Abbot's refutation.

C is "Ex dono authoris", by way of King George III's library.

L, LLP, and LW lack Ff4; LW also lacks ¶1. DT lacks ℓFf.

<u>1624, part of the first reply in a new edition</u>

24 [Within a double rule] A / TREATISE OF THE / Perpetuall Visibilitie, / AND / Succession of the True CHVRCH / <u>in all</u> AGES. / [arms of Abbot as archbishop.] / Printed by <u>Humfrey Lownes</u>, for <u>Robert Milbourne</u>, and are to be sold at his / Shop, at the great South-dore of Saint <u>Paul's</u> Church. / 1624. [Succession, ss is ligature with second s short.]

4°. A-P^4, Q^2. pp. [8], 1-116. 24 lines ℓB-I,
   25 lines ℓK-Q.
      r.t. <u>Of the Visibilite</u> / <u>of the true Church</u>.
         Swash V - ℓK-P1-2, Q1 (versos)
         Italic V - ℓB-I1-4, K-P3-4, Q2 (versos)
         Swash C - ℓB-I3-4, K-O2 (rectos)
         Italic C - ℓB2, C-I1-2, K-O1, 3-4, P1-4,
            Q1-2 (rectos)
         In ℓK-Q the full stop is larger and the
         swash C narrower.

Ala, t.p.: Alb, blank: A2a, "To the reader.": A4b, blank: Bla-Q2b, text.

STC 39.

Seen: L(2 copies) LUC LW BR(c.e.) C(2 copies) CE(c.e.). Not seen: Cartmel Priory Colchester PL Lincoln C Manchester, Rylands Norwich PL Peterborough C Winchester C. [Some may be copies of nos. 24a, b.]

A note in the Bodleian copy of STC 40 (no. 25)
signed W.G. is as follows:

"The whole of this Treatise with the exception
of the last sentence, & the alteration of a few
words relating to Beza on p. 97, is taken word
for word from Dr. (afterwards Abp.) George
Abbot's Reasons wh. Dr. Hill hath brought for
the upholding of Papistry unmasked & c. Oxf.
1604. 4to pp. 25-71.

"Who wrote the preface to this Tract, or why it
represents the Treatise as 'a treasure of
antiquity', 'hard to come by', I know not.

"It is usually attributed to Abp. Abbot as a
distinct treatise. See his life p. 53."

The tract has been erroneously attributed to
James Usher (LW copy of STC 40) and to Daniel
Featley (John Clare: The converted Jew). Laud
in his diary found it hard to credit that
Abbot was the author but seemed pleased that
this was thought to be so. It seems likely
that Abbot did not authorize the publication.
(Trevor-Roper in Archbishop Laud [no. 173]
says with some accuracy that having only cir-
culated in MS at Oxford it was published by
an "enthusiastic supporter".)

Entered in the Register under the hands of Dr.
Featley and Warden Bill on 17 Dec. 1623 (Arber
v. 4, p. 109).

The preface of this issue occupies 13 lines +
3 pages + 18 lines. On A2b, the Greek in the
margin is in large, clear type and is separated
from the marginal note above. On A4a, there is
a marginal note "2 Thes 2."

The running titles show the use of three
formes in printing; the first for both inner
and outer of ⌗B-I (one swash C); the second
for the inner forme of ⌗K-O (one swash C, one
swash V); the third for the outer forme of
⌗K-O and both formes of ⌗P-Q (one swash V.
⌗Q is printed by half-sheet imposition).

LUC lacks the top of the t.p. and has "such
singing & chanting with Organs" on p. 115
crossed through (cf. nos. 24b, 25).

Variant
$C(8.24.19^3)$ has p. 87 misnumbered 88 and also
has "such singing & chanting with Organs" on
p. 115 crossed through.

Another issue

24a [As no. 24 to]/ in all AGES. / [rule] / [foot
of compartment McK. 256, McK. & F. 172] /
[rule] / AT LONDON, / Printed by HVMFREY
LOVVNES, for / ROBERT MILBOVRNE. / 1624.

$4^°$. A-P^4, Q^2. pp. [8], 1-116. 24 lines ⌀B-I,
25 lines ⌀K-Q. r.t. as no. 24.
Error: p. 87 misnumbered 88.

Contents as no. 24.

STC 39 - another issue.

Seen: C   CT   DM   GuPL   O(2 copies)   WF(c.e.).

Variants
i) O(Antiq.e.E.92[3]) has p. 87 correctly
   numbered.
ii) CT has the text of the cancel leaf at Q2
    reading "such pompous Processions with
    banners and reliques" instead of "such sing-
    ing & chanting with Organs, such ringing of
    bells."
iii) WF and DM have p. 87 correctly numbered
     and the cancel leaf at Q2.

Another issue

24b [Titlepage as no. 24a except that there is no
comma after "Lownes".]

$4^°$. A-L^4, M^4 (±M4), N-P^4, Q^2 (±Q2). pp. [8], 1-116
24 lines ⌀B-I, 25 lines ⌀K-Q. r.t. as no. 24
(but see notes below).

A1a, t.p.: A1b, blank: A2a, "To the reader";
"Errata corrige.": B1a-Q2b, text.

STC 39 - another issue.

Seen: LLP.

This copy, from Abbot's library, is bound
before John Perrin's <u>Luther's forerunners</u>
(STC 19769), which for this purpose has a
cancel t.p. "Luther's forerunners: or, a
cloud of witnesses deposing for the Protestant
faith. Gathered together in the historie of
the Waldenses. Whereunto is prefixed, a
Treatise of the perpetuall visibilitie, and
succession of the true Church in all ages.
[device] London, Printed for Nathaneal
Newbery ... 1624."

WF copy listed at 24a is bound after A4 of
this tract, and LW listed at 24 is bound in
the same volume as a copy with the original
titlepage, which is in black and red and re-
places "Whereunto ... ages. [device]" by a
further subtitle.

The link with a history of the Waldenses
appears to be the reason for the cancel leaf
M4, which is only 6 13/16" x 4 13/16 compared
to the normal page size of about 7 3/16" x
5 1/4". The V of "Visibility" in the r.t.
is not swash. Against "Reinerius" on p. 87
is an asterisk denoting a long marginal note
extending over the page quoting from
Reinerius' censure of the Waldenses.

The preface is extended to 13 lines + 4 pages
+ 8 lines by the addition on A2b of a Greek
text and "It is extreame madness (Saith S.
Basil) ... in the earth" after "benefit and
use whereof", and later "not onely whilest
they lived did shine as lights in the middest
of a froward and crooked generation, holding
forth in the world the word of life, but,
also." The Greek in the margin is of rougher
type, close up to the note before, and ending
"&c. Phil. 2.15." The r.t. on A3b and A4b is
"To the **Raeder.**"

On the cancel leaf Q2 the reading is as in no.
24a, variant ii.

"Errata corrige." includes references to
fifteen misprints, all of which appeared in
earlier issues.

1624, part of the first reply in another new edition

25 [As no. 24 to] / in all AGES. / [rule] /
[woodblock: head surrounded by strapwork
^{15}/16" x 2 ^{1}/4"] / [rule] / AT LONDON, /
Printed by AVGVSTINE MATTHEVVES / and IOHN
NORTON, for ROBERT / MILBOVRNE. 1624.

4°. A-P^4. pp.[8], 1-110, [2]. 24 lines $A-B,
    26 lines $C-P.
    r.t. Of the Visibilitie / of the true Church.
       Swash C: $C3-4, E3-4, H4, K4, L3,
          M4, N4, O3, P3 (rectos)
       "true" omitted $D1-2 (rectos)

A1a, t.p.: A1b, blank: A2a, "To the
reader.": B1a, text: P4a-b, blank.

STC 40.

Seen: L LW CE CT DT GuA O   Not seen:
      Lincoln C.

The preface is identical to that in the LLP
copy (no. 24b).

The marginal note on cancellans M4 (pp. 87-88)
of LLP is included on pp. 82-83 of this edition
with a few modifications.

The errata listed in LLP have been corrected.

The troublesome passage on p. 115 of the
earlier edition has been changed to "such
ringing of bells" and is now on p. 110; both
"such singing & chanting with Organs" and
its replacement "such pompous processions
with banners and reliques" have been with-
drawn.

L and O copies lack P4.

The running titles indicate printing from two
formes as follows:

The first for inner ∮L, O, P, outer ∮H, K, M,
N, and both inner and outer ∮B, D, F, I
(error in ∮D - no swash letters).

The second for inner ∮H, K, M, N, outer ∮L,
O, P, and inner and outer ∮C, E, G (one
swash C).

1608.   A SERMON PREACHED AT THE FUNERAL SOLEMNITIES OF THOMAS, EARL OF DORSET

26   A SERMON / PREACHED AT / WESTMINSTER / MAY 26.
1608. / AT / THE FVNERALL SOLEMNITIES / of the
Right Honorable Thomas Earle of / Dorset, late
L. High Treasurer / of ENGLAND. / By GEORGE
ABBOT Doctor of Diuinitie and Deane of
WINCHESTER, one of his Lordships / Chapleines.
/ Now published at the request of some
honourable persons; very / few things being
added, which were then cut off by / the
shortnesse of the time. / IOH. 9.4. / The night
commeth, when no man can worke. / [device: McK.
354a] / LONDON / Printed by Melchisedech
Bradwood for / William Aspley. 1608.

4°. A-E^4. pp. [4], 1-25, [1], 27-32, [4].
    = 40.   37 lines. r.t. on A3b-D3a. A
        funerall Sermon. (Swash A on C2a, D3a.)

A1a, t.p.: A1b, blank: A2a, "To the Rihgt [sic]
Honorable and most vertuous Lady, the La.
Cicely Countesse of Dorset.": A3a, text: D3b,
blank: D4a, "To the reader.": E3a-4b, blank.

STC 38.

Seen: L(2 copies) LG LLP(2 copies) O
    WF(c.e.).

The text of the sermon is Isaiah 40: 6.

In this issue the s of "request" is long.

Entered in the Register 15 June 1608 (Arber
v. 4, p. 381).

L and LLP copies lack E3 and E4.

Another issue

26a [The titlepage is as above except that the st
in "request" is a ligature with short s.]

4°. A-E⁴. pp. [6], 1-25, [1], 27-32, [2].
    = 40. 37 lines. r.t. on A4a-D4a. A
    funerall Sermon. (Swash A on B2a, B3b,
    C1a, C3a, C3b, D1b, D3a.)

A1a-b, blank: A2a, t.p.: A2b, blank: A3a, "To
the Right Honorable and most vertuous Lady,
the La. Cicely Countesse of Dorset.": A4a,
text: D4b, blank: E1a, "To the reader.":
E4a-b, blank.

STC 38 - another issue.

Seen: L(1417.b.22) C.

The text is unchanged.

L lacks A1 and E4.

1608   THE EXAMINATIONS OF GEORGE SPROT

27 [Within a border of arabesque type orns.]
   THE / EXAMINATIONS, / Arraignment & Conuiction
   / of George Sprot, Notary / in Aye-
   mouth, / Together with his constant and /
   extraordinarie behauiour at his / death, in
   Edenborough, / Aug. 12. 1608. / Written & set
   forth by Sir William Hart, / Knight, L.
   Iustice of Scotland. / Whereby appeareth the
   treason- / able device betwixt Iohn late Earle
   of Gowry and Robert Logane of Restalrig /
   (commonly called Lesterig) plotted by / them
   for the cruell murthering / of our most
   gracious Souereigne. / Before which Treatise
   is prefixed / also a Preface, written by G.
   Abbot / Doctour of Diuinitie, and Deane of

Winchester, <u>who was present</u> / <u>at the sayd</u>
Sprots / <u>execution</u>. / [rule] / <u>LONDON</u>: /
Printed by <u>Melch. Bradwood</u>, / for <u>William</u>
<u>Aspley</u>. / 1608.

4°. A-H^4. pp. [2], 1-60, [2]. 26 lines
    (preface): 32 lines (text). r.t.
    on A2b-E4b. THE PREFACE / TO THE READER.
    on F1b-H3b. <u>The Examinations, Arraignment</u>
    / <u>and Conuiction of</u> George Sprot.

A1a, t.p.: A1b, blank: A2a, "A preface to the
reader.": F1a, text: H4a-b, blank.

STC 12894.

Seen: L O   Not seen: DU.

Entered in the Register 10 Nov. 1608 (STC).

The commentator of the <u>Harleian miscellany</u>
(see no. 28) stresses Abbot's obsequiousness
towards the King in his preface.

L copy wants H4.

<u>A reissue</u>

27a [As no. 27 to] / for <u>William Aspley</u>. / 1609.

The format, collation, and contents are identical with those of no. 27.

STC 12894a.

Seen: L C.

Both want H4.

<u>1812 reprint, in collection, of 1609 reissue</u>

28 The examinations, arraignment and conviction
    of George Sprot ... London. Printed by Melch.
    Bradwood, for William Aspley. 1609.

    Appears in:

PARK, Thomas, compiler
The Harleian miscellany: a collection
of scarce, curious and entertaining
pamphlets and tracts, as well in manuscript
as in print. Vol. IX. Being the first
supplemental volume of miscellaneous
pieces, etc. London, White and Cochrane
[etc.], 1812. pp. 560-79.

With introductory matter and footnotes. The
Harleian copy is that now in the British
Museum.

1610?   PRESCRIPT TO THE DIOCESE OF LONDON

29 [A broadsheet]

Heading: To all and euery the Ministers,
Church-wardens, and Side- / men, within the
Citie, Suburbs, and Diocesse of London.

Begin: WHereas I am daily aduertised by the
relations of many and Re- / ligious persons,
of a generall misbehauior in most Churches in,
and about the Citie of London, in time of
diuine Seruice, etc.

End: Whereof both the Lawes / of God, and the
King require a carefull, and religious per-
formance. / GEO: LONDON:

Single sheet, trimmed to 6 3/8" x 10 1/8".
44 lines of text. Neither signatures nor
page number. Verso blank.

LS Catalogue of broadsides, no. 121.

Seen: LS.

1610? is the date assigned to this item by
the LS Catalogue of broadsides, and although
the signature Geo: London: could refer to
Monteigne, the contents are indeed typical
of Abbot, who had been troubled at Oxford by
his congregation's wearing hats in church
and who was always severe on unlicensed
preachers.

<u>1611   BIBLE</u> New Testament. Gospels, Acts,
<u>Revelation.</u> English

30   [Translation of the four Gospels, the Acts of
      the Apostles, and the Revelation of St. John
      the Divine. By Dr. John Perne, Regius pro-
      fessor of Greek and director, Thomas Davis,
      Dr. George Abbot, Richard Eedes, Giles
      Thompson, Sir Henry Savile, Dr. Ralph [?]
      Ravers, and Dr. John Harmer.]

      Appears in:

           BIBLE. <u>English, 1611</u>
              The Holy Bible, conteyning the Old
           Testament, and the new: newly translated
           out of the originall tongues: & with the
           former translations diligently compared and
           reuised, by his Maiesties speciall comande-
           ment. Appointed to be read in Churches.
           Imprinted at London by Robert Barker,
           Printer to the Kings most Excellent Maies-
           tie. 1611. $\int^3$A2a-306a, 3Z4a-3Aa6b.
           STC 2219, <u>etc.</u>

      [The titlepage is engraved. The New Testament
      also has an engraved titlepage: "The Newe
      Testament of our Lord and Sauiour Iesus
      Christ. Newly translated out of the originall
      Greeke: and with the former translations
      diligently compared and reuised, by his
      Maiesties speciall commandement. Imprinted at
      London, <u>etc.</u>"]

      For the order set down for the translating of
      the Bible, see no. 196.

      <u>1622   DIRECTIONS TO PREACHERS</u>, etc.

      Oxford diocese

31   [Woodblock: head and scrolls] / THE COPPIE /
      OF A LETTER SENT / from my Lords Grace of
      Can- / terburie shewing the graue and /
      <u>weighty reasons which induced</u>/ <u>the Kings</u>
      <u>Maiestie to pre-</u> / <u>scribe those former</u> /
      <u>directions for</u> / Preachers. / [device:

McK. 336] / AT OXFORD, / Printed by IOHN
LICHFIELD and/ IAMES SHORT. 1622.

4° A^4 (-A4), *^{4}. No pagination or foliation.
14 pages. 31 lines $A, 32 lines $*. r.t.
None.

Ala, t.p.: Alb, blank: A2a, "To the Right
Reverend Father in God my very good Lord and
Brother the Lord Bishop of Oxon.": *la, "To
the minister churchwardens and parishioners
of [blank] in the Diocesse of Oxon.": *4b,
blank.

STC 33   Madan i. 1622/1 and 1622/6.

Seen: L.

Madan i. 1622/6 is entered under John Howson,
Bishop of Oxford, and consists only of S*,
but Madan doubted if this ever existed as a
genuine separate work.

Madan also conjectured that A4 was blank.

This work originated in James I's alarm at the
number of preachers of all shades of opinion,
particularly of those who neared the Protestantism that he had experienced in Scotland.

The letter which begins on Ala is by Abbot
and is dated from Croydon, 4 Sept. 1622. It
is the same letter that was sent by him to
all the bishops of his province explaining
the directions for preachers. It begins
(after the greeting) "I doubt not but ..."

The letter which begins on *la is that sent by
John Howson, Bishop of Oxford, to his
parochial clergy. He first introduces the
letter he has received from Abbot which contained the King's original letter of 4 Aug.
1622 to the Archbishop (beginning "Forasmuch
as the abuses"). Abbot sent this to his suf-
fragans on 12 Aug. 1622. Next Howson introduces and commends the directions. This
letter is dated from Oxford, 31 Aug. 1622.

Norwich diocese

32   [No titlepage; the contents are described
      more fully.]

      4°. A^4. pp. [3], 2-6. 39 lines. r.t. None.

      A1a-b, blank: A2a, "[type orns.] / The Kings
      MAIESTIES Letter to the Lords / <u>Grace</u> of
      <u>Canterbury</u>, touching <u>Preaching</u>, / and
      <u>Preachers</u>.": A3b-4b, "[type orns.] / The Lord
      Archbishop of <u>Canterburie</u> his Letters/ to the
      Bishop of the Diocesse of Norwich."

      Erroneously equated with STC 33.

      Seen: CE DU(c.e.).

      The letter which starts on A2a is the King's
      letter of 4 Aug. 1622.

      The letter which starts on A3b is Abbot's
      letter of 4 Sept. 1622, as sent to the Bishop
      of Oxford.

      There is no date or imprint.

      DU lacks A1.

      <u>1642   To the Archbishop of York and the
      Lord Keeper</u>

33   KING / JAMES / HIS LETTER / AND / DIRECTIONS
      TO THE / LORD ARCHBISHOP / OF CANTERBURY; /
      Concerning Preaching and Preachers; / <u>With</u> /
      <u>the</u> / Bishop of <u>Canterburies</u> Letter to the /
      Bishop of <u>Lincolne</u>, Lord Keeper, desiring /
      him to put in practise the Kings desires,
      that / none should preach but in a Religious
      forme. / And not that every young man should
      / take to himselfe an exorbitant Liberty, to
      / preach what he listeth, to the offence of
      **his Ma- / jesty, and the disturbance and
      disquiet** of the / **Church and Common-wealth.**
      / [rule] / Printed for <u>**Thomas Walkeley**</u>, 1642.

      4°. A^4, B^2. pp. [2], 1-9, [1]. 36 lines. r.t.
      None.

A1a, t.p.: A1b, blank: A2a, "King James his
letter ... concerning preaching and
preachers.": A2b, 1. 25, "His Majesties orders
and directions, concerning preaching and
preachers.": A4a, 1. 6, "The Arch-Bishop of
Canterburies Letter, to the Arch-Bishop of
Yorke.": B1b, 1. 9, "The Lord-Arch-Bishops
Letter, to the Lord Keeper.": B2b, blank.

Wing J139   Thomason E.147(17).

Seen: L O   Not seen: L-Lincoln's Inn
    E - National Library of Scotland.

The King's letter is that of 4 Aug. 1622, with
the articles; the letter from Abbot to Tobias
Matthew, Archbishop of York, is that of 4 Sept.
1622. The letter to the Lord Keeper, John
Williams, Bishop of Lincoln, is in the same
vein but shorter, beginning "By this you
see ... "

<u>1642</u>   To the Archbishop of York and
the Lord Keeper

34 REMARKEABLE / PASSAGES: / <u>FIRST</u>, / A prayer
    for the Parliament. / <u>AS ALSO</u> / THE ARCH-
    BISHOP OF / Canterburies Letter to the Arch-
    / Bishop of <u>Yorke</u>, and the Lord Keeper, to /
    put in Practice the Kings desires. / WITH A
    PETITION TO / His Majestie, by divers
    Noblemen / and Gentlemen estated in Ireland,
    and now / residing in <u>London</u>. / <u>ALSO</u> / A NEW
    DECLARATION FROM / Both Houses of <u>Parliament</u>.
    / <u>Ordered by the Lords and Commons in</u>
    <u>Parliament, that this be forthwith</u> / Printed.
    / Hen. Elsying. Cler. Par. D. Com / [rule] /
    Printed for W.G. 1642. / <u>Iuly</u> 15.

4°. 4 unsigned, unnumbered leaves in one
    gathering. 39 lines. r.t. None.

1a, t.p.: 1b, 1. 1, "A praier for the High
Court of Parliament." - 1. 24, "The Arch-
Bishop of Canterburies Letter, to the Arch-
Bishop of Yorke.": 3a, 1. 8, "The Lord Arch-
Bishops Letter to the Lord Keeper." - 1. 27,

"To the Kings most Excellent Maiestie.": 4a,
l. 20-4b, "A new declaration from both Houses
of Parliament."

Wing R922   Thomason E.155(17).

Seen: L DN.

The letters are the same as those in the pre-
vious entry (no. 33) except that the King's
letter is omitted, as are also the articles.
This work seems to be a tract of government
propaganda, and the titlepage, significantly,
does not mention Abbot. Perhaps the
publishers hoped that Laud's name would be
understood.

1654, reprinted in collection

35   The Archbishop of Canterbury to the Bishops
     concerning King James his directions for
     preachers, with the Directions, Aug. 15, 1622.
     [sic for 12 Aug.].

     Appears in:

         CABALA: sive scrinia sacra. Mysteries of
             state and government: in letters of
             illustrious persons ... In two parts,
             etc. London, printed for G. Bedel and
             T. Collins, 1654. pt. 2, pp. 183-86.
             Wing C184.

     There are later editions.

     The text is Abbot's commendation of the King's
     letter of 4 Aug. 1622, with the letter.

     This is also printed in pt. 2, pp. 190-92, the
     letter beginning "I doubt not before this time
     you will have received ... the directions"
     claiming to be from the Bishop of Lincoln
     (John Williams) to the Bishop of London
     (George Monteigne), dated 3 Sept. 1622. This
     letter is reprinted in Collier's Ecclesiasti-
     cal History (no. 152), v. 2, p. 724 (new
     edition, v. 7, pp. 431-34).

1737, reprinted in collection

36   The King's letter to the Archbishop of Canter-
      bury concerning preachers and preaching. Reg.
      II. Abbot. fol. 109. a. - Directions concern-
      ing preachers. - The Archbishop of Canter-
      bury's letter explaining the former direc-
      tions. Reg. II. Abbot fol. 200. a.

      Appears in:

           WILKINS, David, compiler
              Concilia. [No. 251.] v. 4, pp. 465-67.

      The letters do not refer to a specific
      diocese. The first text is of Abbot's com-
      mendation of the King's letter of 4 Aug. 1622,
      with the letter.

      1839, reprinted in collection

37   [a] The King's letter to the Archbishop of
           Canterbury concerning preachers and
           preaching. - Reg. II. Abbot fol. 199a.

      [b] Directions concerning preachers.

      [c] The Archbishop of Canterbury's letter ex-
           plaining the former directions. - Reg. II.
           Abbot. fol. 200. a. [Croydon, 4 Sept.
           1622].

      Appears in:

           CARDWELL, Edward, D.D.
              Documentary annals of the reformed
           Church of England ... from the year 1546
           to the year 1716: with notes historical
           and explanatory, by Edward Cardwell.
           Oxford, University Press, 1839. v. 2,
           pp. 133-34.

      [a] is printed with Abbot's introduction and
      commendation to his bishops from Croydon, 12
      Aug. 1622. The letters do not refer to a
      specific diocese.

1626   SUPPORT FOR SUBSIDY TO THE KING OF
DENMARK

38 [Introductory sentence and concluding commen-
    dation, dated Croydon, 26 Sept. 1626.]

Appears in:

    CHARLES I
        Instructions directed from the Kings
    Most Excellent Maiestie. [No. 267.]
    ₰A2a, B3a-b.

    WILKINS, David, compiler
        Concilia. [No. 251.] v. 4, pp. 471, 473.

    CARDWELL, Edward, D.D.
        Documentary annals of the reformed
    Church of England. [See no. 37.] v. 2,
    pp. 158, 164.

1631   CONTRIBUTION TO FOX'S MARTYRS

39 A true narration of a bloodie massacre com-
    mitted vpon the Protestants by the Papists
    in the greater part of the Valtoline in the
    yeare 1620, after the new stile: published
    for a necessarie admonition to all estates,
    wherein the Gospell is professed amongst the
    Papists, and for an example to all true
    Christians of Constancie in the profession
    of the Holy Gospell. [B.L.]

Appears in:

    FOXE, John, the martyrologist
        The third volume of the ecclesiastical
    historie: containing the acts and
    monuments of martyrs ... Recogniaed and
    inlarged by the Author Iohn Foxe. Where-
    unto are annexed certaine additions, vnto
    the time of our Soueraigne Lord King
    Charles now raigning. [Seventh edition.]
    London, printed by R. Young, 1631. ff.
    [sic, for pp.] 98-105 of the additional
    matter after ₰4Q. STC 11228.

[Between 4Q4b and 4R1a are 106 pp. separately
signed and paged with the additional t.p. "A
continuation of the histories of forrein
martyrs: from the happy reigne of the most re-
nowned Qu. Elizabeth, to these times ...
Together with the barbarous cruelties exer-
cised vpon the professors of the Gospell in
the Valtoline, 1621. London, printed by Adan
Islip, Foelix Kingston, and Robert Young,
1632."]

Many later editions not inspected.

For the attribution to Abbot, see Wood, Watt,
BB, DNB, etc. Six chapters appear under the
heading given above, and at the end is
"Signes and prodigies, which happened before
the massacre in the Valtoline", but only the
first of the chapters concerns this massacre.
None of my sources tells whether Abbot wrote
only this short first chapter or the whole
section, pp. 98-106.

B   POSTHUMOUSLY PUBLISHED WORKS (INCLUDING
      RELEVANT LETTERS AND SPEECHES)

I   The Essex divorce case

      <u>1613</u>?

40   Some memorials touching the nullity between
      the Earl of Essex and his lady, pronounced
      September 25, 1613, at Lambeth, and the diffi-
      culties endured in the same.

      12°. pp. 56.

      This work, with the above details, is men-
      tioned in the BB article, but it is unrecorded
      elsewhere and I have not traced a copy.

      <u>1651</u>

41   His G. Arguments. The Lord Archbishop his
      speech to his Majesty.

      Appears in:

           **The NARRATIVE history of King James, for
           the first fourteen years. In four parts
           etc. London, printed for Michael Sparke,
           <u>1651</u>. pp. 95-100. Wing S4818.**

      [There is an additional titlepage at p. 87 as
      follows: "Truth brought to light by time.
      The proceedings touching the divorce between
      the Lady Frances Howard, and Robert Earl of
      Essex, before the Kings Delegate, George
      Canterbury, Iohn Bishop of London, Lancelot
      Bishop of Ely, Richard Bishop of Lichfeild
      and Coventry, Doctor ACaesar, Thomas Parrey,
      Dr. Donne, John Bennet, Frances James, and
      Thomas Edwards, authorized under the Kings
      Broad seale: with his Majesties answer, etc."]

This part of the four-part <u>Narrative history</u>
contains "Allegations made," Essex's reply,
"Doubts conceived out of the fact and process
of the suit," "His G. Arguments," the King's
answer, "The commissioners that gave sentence," "The commissioners dissenting," and
other connected trials.

Reprinted in:

> SCOTT, <u>Sir</u> Walter, <u>Bart</u>., <u>compiler</u>
> A collection of scarce and valuable
> tracts, on the most interesting and en-
> tertaining subjects ... selected from an
> infinite number in print and manuscript,
> in the Royal, Cotton, Sion and other
> libraries ... particularly that of the
> late Lord Somers. The Second edition, re-
> vised, <u>etc</u>. London, Cadell [etc.], 1809.
> v. 2, pp. 307-10.

The whole tract is reprinted.

<u>1711</u>

42 The Lord Archbishop of Canterbury [reasons
against the nullity].

Appears in:

> HOWARD, <u>Lady</u> Frances, <u>Countess of Essex</u>
> The case of insufficiency discus'd,
> being the proceedings at large, touching
> the divorce between the Lady Frances Howard
> and Robert Earl of Esses ... With the
> arguments on both sides; also that learned
> speech of Dr. George Abbot, Archbishop of
> Canterbury, against the Countess, and the
> King's answer thereunto. London: Printed
> for E. Curll, 1711. pp. 7-10.

The contents of the whole book are as the 1651
<u>Narrative history</u> with the addition of a list
of authorities cited by Abbot, a copy of the
divorce, "An account of the intrigue between
Robert Carr and the Lady Frances Howard"
[from Arthur Wilson's <u>History of Great</u>

Britain], and an appendix. The trials of
those involved in the poisoning of Overbury
are omitted.

<u>1715</u>

43   THE / CASE / OF / IMPOTENCY. / As Debated in
ENGLAND, / In that Remarkable TRYAL An. /
1613. between ROBERT, Earl of / ESSEX, and the
Lady FRANCES / HOWARD, who, after Eight Years
Marriage, commenc'd a Suit against / him for
IMPOTENCY. / CONTAINING / I. The whole
PROCEEDINGS, and DEBATES / on both sides. /
II. The REPORT of the Seven MATRONS /
appointed to search the <u>Countess</u>. / III. The
Intrigue between Her and the / Earl of
SOMERSET, who after the Divorce mar- / ried
her. / IV. A Detection of some Politicks in
the / Court of King JAMES the First. / [rule]
/ Written by GEORGE ABBOT, D.D. / Lord
Archbishop of Canterbury. / [rule] / In Two
VOLUMES. / [rule] / <u>London</u>, Printed for <u>E</u>.
<u>Curll</u>, at the <u>Dial</u> and <u>Bible</u> / against <u>St</u>.
<u>Dunstan's</u> Church in Fleetstreet. 1715. /
Price Five Shillings.

I. 12°. π_A^4, A-H^{12}, I^2. pp. [10], 3-196.
        Portrait of Carr and Lady Frances
        Howard. 30-32 lines.
        r.t. A2b-D12a: <u>The CASE of the E. of</u>
             <u>ESSEX / And the Lady HOWARD</u>.
             E1b-G12a: <u>The Case of the Earl of</u>
             <u>ESSEX / and the Lady HOWARD</u>.
             G12b-I2b: <u>The Case of the Earl of</u>
             <u>SOMERSET / and the Countess of ESSEX</u>.

Plate: πA1a, t.p.: πA1b, blank: πA2a, "The
preface": πA3a, "Some account of Archbishop
Abbot.": πA4a, "The contents of this volume.":
A1a, "The case of Robert, Earl of Essex; and
the Lady Frances Howard, written by Archbishop Abbot, printed from his Grace's
original manuscript.": A1b, blank: A2a, "Some
memorials touching the nullity between the
Earl of Essex and his Lady, pronounc'd Sept.
25, 1613, at Lambeth, and the difficulties
endur'd in the same." [By Abbot, 2 Oct. 1613]:

C6a, "Some observable things since September
25, 1613.": D12b, blank: E1a, "The speech intended to be spoken at Lambeth, September 25,
1613. By the Archbishop of Canterbury, when it
came to his turn to declare his mind concerning the nullity of marriage between the Earl
of Essex, and the Lady Frances Howard.": F6b,
"The King's letter to the Archbishop of Canterbury.": F8b, "The libel promoted by the
Lady Frances Howard against Robert, Earl of
Essex.": F10b, "The Earl of Essex replieth.":
F11b, "Doubts conceived out of the fact and
process of the suit.": F12a, "The Lord Archbishop of Canterbury's reasons against the
nullity.": G1b, authorities cited by Abbot:
G9b, the commissioners' sentence: G10b, "The
copy of the divorce.": G11b, "An account of
the intrigue between Robert Carr and Lady
Frances Howard." [By Arthur Wilson]: H9a-I2b,
"The countess's attempts against the earl, by
sorcery."

The BB article states that "Some observable
things" was written either by Abbot or at his
direction.

<u>1719</u>

44   THE / CASE / OF / IMPOTENCY, / As Debated in
ENGLAND, / In that Remarkable TRYAL, 1613. /
between ROBERT Earl of Essex, and the / Lady
FRANCES HOWARD who, after / Eight Years
Marriage, commenc'd a Suit / against him for
IMPOTENCY. / CONTAINING / I. The whole
PROCEEDINGS and DEBATES / on both sides. /
II. The REPORT of the Seven MATRONS /
appointed to search the <u>Countess</u>. / III. The
Intrigue between Her and the / Earl of
SOMERSET, who after the Di- / vorce married
her. / IV. A Detection of some Politicks in
the / Court of King JAMES the First. / [rule]
/ Written by GEORGE ABBOT, <u>D.D.</u> Lord /
Archbishop of <u>Canterbury</u>, / [rule] / In Two
VOLUMES. / [rule] / The THIRD EDITION. /
[rule] / <u>LONDON</u>, Printed for E. CURLL, at the
<u>Dyal and</u> / <u>Bible</u> in <u>Fleetstreet</u>. 1719.
⟨Price 5s.⟩

12°. A⁴, B-I¹². pp. [9], 2-192. 32 lines. r.t.
The CASE of the E. of ESSEX, / And the Lady
HOWARD.

The contents are identical in text and
arrangement with those of the 1715 edition
save for readjustments because of the reduced
number of pages.

Volume 2 of the work is unconnected with the
case.

1719

45   The proceedings between the Lady Frances
Howard and Robert Earl of Essex, before the
King's Delegates, George Archbishop of Canter-
bury [and others] ... authoriz'd under the
King's Broad-seal. Anno 1613. 11 Jac. 1.

Appears in:

A COMPLEAT collection of state-tryals and
proceedings upon impeachments for high
treason, and other crimes and mis-
demeanours; from the reign of King
Henry the Fourth, to the end of the
Reign of Queen Anne, etc. London,
printed for Timothy Goodwin [etc.],
1719. v. 1, pp. 223-228.

Includes "The allegations," Essex's answers,
"Doubts conceived," "His G. Arguments," the
King's answer, and a brief notice of the
sentence.

This work went to several enlarged editions
before being entirely revised as the next
work.

1809

46   Proceedings between the Lady Frances Howard,
Countess of Essex, and Robert Earl of Essex,
her husband before the King's Delegates, in a
cause of divorce: 11 James I. A.D. 1613.

Appears in:

> COBBETT, William, M.P., compiler
> Cobbett's Complete collection of state
> trials and proceedings for high treason
> and other crimes and misdemeanors from the
> earliest period to the present time.
> London, R. Bagshaw, 1809. v. 2, cols.
> 785-862.

Includes the material in no. 45 with an
account headed "The foregoing account of the
proceedings between the Earl of Essex and Lady
Frances Howard being but short and very im-
perfect ... the following account, written by
Dr. George Abbot ... with the Speech he in-
tented to have made and King James' letter to
him, will throw much light upon that affair
and help greatly to explain it."

II   The shooting accident

1698

47   A short apologie for Arch-bishop Abbot, touching the death of Peter Hawkins. By an unknown
hand. With a large answer to this apologie,
by Sir Henry Spelman Kt. As also, several
letters relating to the same fact: with a copy
of the dispensation for irregularity, granted
to the Arch-bishop, etc.

Appears in:

> SPELMAN, Sir Henry
> Reliquae Spelmannianae. The posthumous
> works of Sir Henry Spelman Kt. relating to
> the laws and antiquities of England, etc.
> Oxford, printed at the Theatre for Awnsham
> and John Churchill, 1698. pp. 106-26. Wing
> S4930.

The letters are from the King to Bishop
Williams and others, 3 Oct. 1621; from
Williams and others to Abbot, 5 Oct. 1621;
Abbot's reply, 13 Oct. 1621, with footnotes by
Williams; the opinion of Williams and others

sent to the King 10 Nov. 1621.

Edmund Gibson, the editor, states in the preface that Abbot and Laud were the chief
influences upon Spelman to publish his Concilia. The text of the Apology and the
Answer, both in Spelman's hand, were originally in the possession of Spelman's grand-
son; but most authorities believe Abbot
wrote his own Apology. The letters had
passed from Archbishop Sancroft to Henry
Wharton and Richard Chiswell. John Hacket
claimed to have seen the Apology in Abbot's
own hand.

See also no. 261.

1723

48 A short apologie for Archbishop Abbot, touching the death of Peter Hawkins. By an unknown
hand. With a large answer to this Apology by
Sir Henry Spelman Kt. As also, several
letters relating to the same fact: with a
copy of the dispensation for irregularity,
granted to the Archbishop, etc.

Appears in:

SPELMAN, Sir Henry
The English works of Sir Henry Spelman,
Kt. Publish'd in his lifetime; together
with his posthumous works ... Now revised,
etc. London: printed for D. Browne, sen &
jun, W. Mears, F. Clay. 1723. pt. 2, pp.
105-26.

The text is the same as that of 1698. A
second edition appeared in 1727.

1809

49 Proceedings against George Abbot, Archbishop
of Canterbury, for the killing of Edward
[sic] Hawkins, one of Lord Zouch's Keepers.
19 James I. A.D. 1621.

Appears in:

> COBBETT, William, M.P., compiler
> Cobbett's Complete collection of state
> trials. [See no. 46.] v. 2, cols. 1159-84.

The contents as in Spelman, with an introduction.

1839

50 A short apologie for Archbishop Abbot, etc.

Appears in:

> CARDWELL, Edward, D.D.
> Documentary annals of the reformed
> Church of England. [See no. 37.] v. 2,
> pp. 135-40.

Reprints the text in Spelman with notes.

III Archbishop Abbot's sequestration

1659

51 Archbishop Abbot, his narrative ... penned
with his own hand, and left to posterity.

Appears in:

> RUSHWORTH, John, M.A., compiler
> Historical collections ... beginning
> the sixteenth year of King James, anno
> 1618. and ending the fifth year of King
> Charles, anno 1629. Digested in order of
> time, and now published by John Rushworth,
> London, printed by Thomas Newcomb for
> George Thomason, 1659. pp. 434-57. Wing
> R2316.

1681

52   Archbishop Abbot his narrative.

Appears in:

    [FRANKLAND, Thomas, M.D.]
      The annals of King James and King
    Charles the First, both of happy memory.
    Containing a faithful history, and impar-
    tial account of the great affairs of state
    and transactions of parliaments in England
    from [1612 to 1642], etc. London, printed
    by Tho. Braddyll for Robert Clavel, 1681.
    pp. 212-24. Wing F2078.

1809

53   The case of George Abbot, Archbishop of Can-
    terbury for refusing to license a sermon
    preached by Dr. Sibthorp, in order to promote
    the loan, and to justify the king's imposing
    public taxes without consent of Parliament.
    3 Charles I. A.D. 1627. ⟨1 Rushw. Coll.
    422-431.⟩

Appears in:

    COBBETT, William, M.P., compiler
      Cobbett's Complete collection of state
    trials. [See no. 46.] v. 2, cols. 1449-80.

With an introduction and the Commission to
Sequester Abbot.

1882

54   The sequestration of Archbishop Abbot from
    all his ecclesiastical offices, in 1627. John
    Rushworth, Esq., of Lincoln's Inn. ⟨Histori-
    cal Collections, i, 435. Ed. 1659.⟩ - Arch-
    bishop Abbot's own narrative. ⟨Rushworth.
    Historical Collections, idem.⟩

Appears in:

ARBER, Edward, compiler
An English garner: ingatherings from our history and literature by Edward Arber, etc. Birmingham, E. Arber, 1882. v. 4, pp. 535-76.

With a very favourable introduction on Abbot and the Commission to Sequester Abbot.

Reprinted in:

[ARBER, Edward, compiler]
An English garner: Stuart tracts, 1603-1693. With an introduction by C.H. Firth. Westminster, Constable, 1903. pp. 309-50.

1600/01   TO THE CITIZENS OF LONDON

55   Cheap-side Crosse / censured and condemned /
BY / A LETTER SENT / From the Vicechancellour
and / other Learned Men of the fa- / mous
Vniversitie of Oxford, / in answer to a
question propounded / by the Citizens of
London, concern- / ing the said CROSSE, in
the / yeere 1600, in which yeer / it was
beautified, / As also some divine Arguments
taken out of / a Sermon against the CROSSE,
a little after / it was last repaired, / By
a learned and godly Minister, sometimes /
Preacher at Alhallows Lombardstreet. / 2
CHRON. 31. 1. / All Israel that were present
went out to the Cities of Iudah, / and brake
the images in pieces &c, untill they had ut-
/ terly destroyed them all. / [rule] /
LONDON, / Printed by A.N. for I.R. and are to
be sold at his / Shop in Pauls Church-yard,
1641.

4°. A-B⁴. pp. [2], 1-14. 33 lines. r.t. None.

A1a, t.p.: A1b, blank: A2a, text: B3a, "The
approbation of Master Vicechancellor's
Letter, by five other learned men, etc.":
B4a, Archer, the minister's sermon: B4b,
conclusion.

Wing A64   Thomason E.100(2)   Madan ii. 979.

Seen: L(E.100[2]) LG(A.7.6.40).

Abbot was Vice-Chancellor of Oxford in 1600,
and his name appears in the headtitle. As
usual, he was prolix, and the sponsors of
this pamphlet, issued as wrath was again boil-
ing up over Cheapside Cross, summarized some
of his argument on pp. 8-9.

Thomason acquired this on 29 April 1643 and changed the imprint to 1643. It seems to have been reissued just as the Cross was actually removed on 2 May 1643.

This pamphlet exists in several issues and states, there being several variations in the heaviness of impression of certain letters, but nothing consistent. All the titlepages, even when their text is the same, are re-settings of the type.

There are two definite variants in the text between states.
i) On B1b, in the marginal note, "off he" or "off the" & "Take / notice of the zeale of the Prelate in this businesse" or "Take notice of the blinde zeale of the Prelate in this businesse."
ii) On B4b, l.1 of para. 2 "man" or "mian."

Another issue

55a [As no. 55 to] repaired, / By a learned and godly Minister, <u>M. Iohn Archer</u>, som- / times Preacher at <u>Alhallows Lombardstreet</u>. / about sixteen years past. / 2 CHRON. 31. 1. / [then as no. 55 except for no hyphen after "ut"].

Format, collation, pagination, and contents as no. 55.

Wing A64 - another issue.

Seen: L(101.i.30) O(Gough 148).

L(101.i.30) has "off he," "zeale," and "man."

O(Gough 148) has "off the," "blinde zeale," and "mian."

Another issue

55b [As no. 55 to] repaired, / By that learned and godly Minister, Mr. <u>Iohn Archer</u>, /

sometimes Preacher at <u>Alhallows</u>
<u>Lombardstreet</u>. / about sixteen years
past. / 2 CHRON. 31. 1. / [then as
no. 55a].

Format, collation, pagination, and contents
as no. 55.

Wing A64 - another issue.

Seen: O(Wood 514).

This issue has "off he," "zeale," and "mian."

<u>Another issue</u>

55c [As no. 55 to] beautified, / As also a
remarkable passage to the same pur-
/pose, in a Sermon preached to an eminent and
very / great Auditory in this City of <u>London</u>:
by a / very reverend, holy, and learned Di-
/ vine a while after the Crosse / was last
repaired, which / was <u>Anno</u>. 1606. / 2 CHRON.
31.1. / [then as no. 55 except for comma after
"ut" instead of hyphen].

Format, collation, pagination, and contents
as no. 55.

Wing A63   Thomason E135(41).

Seen: L (E.135[41]) LG(AZ6.41)   LW
   O(Gough 282 and 4° Z Jur).   Not seen:
   L-Victoria and Albert L-St. Paul's.

LW and O(Gough 282) have "off he," "zeale,"
and "man."

L(E.135[41]) and O(4° Z Jur) have "off the,"
"blinde zeale," and "main."

LG has "off he," "zeale," and "mian."

24 NOV. 1611   TO THE BISHOP OF PETERBOROUGH
(THOMAS DOVE)

56 Archbishop Abbot's letter to the Bishop of
    Peterborough, touching and restraining Mr.
    Dodd, and other nonconformists, from preaching.

    Appears in:

        COLLIER, Jeremy, the Nonjuror
           An ecclesiastical history of Great
        Britain. [No. 152.] v. 2, p. ^{2}107.
        (New edition, v. 9, p. 371.)

21 JAN. 1611/12   TO LORD ELLESMERE

57 Execution of Legate and Wightman.

    Appears in:

        COLLIER, John Payne, editor
           The Egerton papers: a collection of
        public and private documents ... from the
        original manuscripts, the property of the
        Right Hon. Lord Francis Egerton. London,
        Camden Society, 1840. (Old Series, 19.)
        pp. 446-47.

    With facsimile signature of Abbot and ex-
    planatory text.

    and in:

        HOOK, Walter Farquharson, Dean of
           Chichester
           Lives of the archbishops of Canterbury.
        [No. 166.] v. 10, pp. 268-69.

22 JAN. 1611/12   TO LORD ELLESMERE

58 Choice of the judges [for the trials of
Legate and Wightman].

Appears in:

> COLLIER, John Payne, editor
>   The Egerton papers. [See no. 57.]
> pp. 447-48.

> HOOK, Walter Farquharson, Dean of
>   Chichester
>   Lives of the archbishops of Canterbury.
> [No. 166.] v. 10, p. 209.

12 MARCH 1611/12   TO SIR RALPH WINWOOD

59 Archbishop Abbot to Sir Ralph Winwood. 12
March 1611/12. [On Mr. Amias, an English
separatist preacher at the Hague.]

Appears in:

> WINWOOD, Sir Ralph
>   Memorials of affairs of state in the
> reigns of Q. Elizabeth and K. James I.
> Collected (chiefly) from the original
> papers of the Rt. Hon. Sir Ralph Winwood.
> London, printed by W.B. for T. Ward,
> 1725. v. 3, pp. 346-47.

22 JULY 1612   TO JAMES I

60 Abbot, Lord archbishop of Canterbury, to King
James; informing his majesty of secret
treasonable practices of Sunega, the Spanish
ambassador, anno. 1612.

Appears in:

> STRYPE, John
>   Brief annals of the Church and State
> ... being a continuation of the Annals.
> [Annals of the Reformation, etc., v. 4.]
> London, printed for Edward Symon, 1731.
> p. 404. (Later edition, Oxford, Univer-
> sity Press, 1824. v. 4, p. 564.)

<u>1 DEC. 1612</u>   <u>TO THE BISHOP OF NORWICH</u>
(JOHN JEGON)

61   [Concerning William Sayer. An extract of the
letter.]

Appears in:

> BURRAGE, Champlin
>   The early English dissenters in the
> light of recent research, 1550-1641.
> Cambridge, University Press, 1912.
> v. 2, pp. 170-71.

The original letter is Cambridge University
Library Add MS. Mm. 6.58. f. 181.

<u>25 FEB. 1612/13</u>   <u>TO THE ARCHBISHOP OF DUBLIN</u>
(THOMAS JONES)

62   [Concerning Irish Church uniformity. An extract from the letter.]

Appears in:

> USHER, James, <u>Archbishop of Armagh</u>
>   The whole works of the Most Rev. James
> Ussher ... With a life of the author ...
> by Charles Richard Elrington. Dublin,
> Hodges and Smith: London, Whittaker, 1847.
> v. 1, pp. 32-33.

1 JUNE 1613   TO SIR RALPH WINWOOD

63   Archbishop Abbot to Sir Ralph Winwood. Lam-
     beth, 1st June 1613. [On Grotius.]

     Appears in:

        WINWOOD, Sir Ralph
           Memorials. [See no. 59.] v. 3, pp.
        460-61.

        BIOGRAPHIA BRITANNICA. [See no. 156.]
           v. 1, p. 9.

OCTOBER 1613   TO JAMES I

--   All letters concerning the Essex divorce case
     are listed in section B, since they are often
     combined with Abbot's narrative.

     Besides the arguments used by Abbot at the
     trial and the narrative known in no. 43 as
     "The case of Robert, Earl of Essex and the
     Lady Frances Howard", Abbot also wrote on
     2 Oct. 1613 "Some memorials touching the
     nullity between the Earl of Essex and his
     Lady", for which see nos. 40, 42-46. He
     also sent to the King the text of the speech
     he never had a chance to make because the
     case had gone against him and he had been ex-
     cused from his place on the commission; for
     this letter see nos. 41-46.

     For letters by others, see part II, section
     E.

JUNE 1614   TO THE BISHOPS OF LONDON AND
NORWICH (JOHN KING AND JOHN JEGON)

64   The Archbishop of Canterbury to the Bishop of
     London. ⟨Desires him to assist in raising a
     loan for the king, upon the Parliament refus-
     ing it.⟩ Lambeth, the ... of June 1614.

Appears in:

> GOODMAN, Godfrey, <u>Bishop of Gloucester</u>
> The court of James the first, to which
> are added letters illustrative of the per-
> sonal history of the most distinguished
> characters in the court of the monarch ...
> Now first published from the original
> manuscripts by John S. Brewer. London,
> Bentley, 1839. v. 2, pp. 157-60.

> TANNER, Joseph Robson, <u>editor</u>
> Constitutional documents of the reign
> of James I, 1603-1625, with an historical
> commentary by J.R. Tanner. Cambridge,
> University Press, 1930. pp. 326-63.

> SPEDDING, James
> The letters and life of Francis Bacon.
> [See no. 163.] v. 3, pp. 78-79.

In Goodman and Tanner the letter is to the
Bishop of London, in Spedding to the Bishop
of Norwich.

<u>17 SEPT. 1614</u>   <u>TO JOHN MURRAY</u>

65   The Archbishop of Canterbury to John Murray,
September 17, 1614. [On an attempt to convert
a Mr. Dorrels from Roman Catholicism.]

Appears in:

> MAIDMENT, James, <u>editor</u>
> Letters and state papers, during the
> reign of King James the Sixth. Chiefly
> from the manuscript collections of Sir
> James Balfour of Denmyln. Edinburgh,
> Abbotsford Club, 1838. (<u>Publications</u>, 13.)
> pp. 231-32.

<u>13 DEC. 1614</u>   <u>TO THE CORPORATION OF</u>
<u>GUILDFORD</u>

66   A worthy and memorable letter, received from
the Lord of Canterbury his Grace. From

Lambeth. Dec. 13. 1614. [On endowments for Guildford.]

Appears in:

> RUSSELL, John, editor
>   The life of Dr. George Abbot. [No. 157.]
> pp. 73-76.

> [RUSSELL, John, editor]
>   The history of Guildford, etc. Guild-
> ford, J. and S. Russell [etc.], 1801.
> pp. 10-16.

10 DEC. 1615   TO SIR GEORGE VILLIERS

67 Archbishop Abbot to Sir George Villiers,
    afterwards Duke of Buckingham. <Upon his
    rise at Court.>

Appears in:

> GOODMAN, Godfrey, Bishop of Gloucester
>   The court of James the first. [See
> no. 64.] v. 2, pp. 160-61.

23 JULY 1616   TO THE ARCHBISHOP OF ST. ANDREWS (JOHN SPOTTISWOODE)

68 The Archbishop of Canterbury to the Arch-
    bishop of St. Andrews [on the absolution
    of the Marquis of Huntley in England].

Appears in:

> SPOTTISWOODE, John, Archbishop of Glasgow
>   and of St. Andrew's
>
>   The history of the Church of Scotland,
> beginning the Year of our Lord 203, and
> continued to the end of the reign of King
> James the VI., etc. London, printed by J.
> Flesher for R. Royster, 1655. pp. 527-28.
> (Later edition, Edinburgh, for the Spot-
> tiswoode Society, 1847-51; Bannatyne Club
> Publication, 93, v. 3, pp. 233-35.)

[LANG, David, editor]
Original letters relating to the ecclesiastical affairs of Scotland. [No. 217.]
pp. 476-78.

17 NOV. 1617   TO CYRIL LUCARIS, PATRIARCH
OF ALEXANDRIA

69   Georgius Abbat, divina providentia Archiepis-
copus Cantuariensis totius Angliae Primus &
Metropolitanus sanctissimo domino, & fratri,
Cyrillo, Papae & patriarchae Alexandrino, &
Iudici oe cumenico, in Christo salutem. [A
translation of this Latin letter is also
given. An answer to Cyril's letter of
friendship of 1 March 1617, which is also
printed in Latin and English.]

Appears in:

PAGITT, Ephraim
Christianographie, or the description
of the multitude and sundry sorts of
Christians in the VVorld not subject to
the Pope, etc. London, printed by T.P.
and W.J. for Matthew Costerden,
Stationer, 1635. $Hh4a-Ii3b.

JUNE-SEPT. 1618   TO NATHANIEL BRENT

70   [a]   To my very loving friend Mr. Nathaniel
Brent at the House of Mr. Daniel Nice,
give these ... Lambeth, June 12. 1618.
[b]   To my very loving friend Mr. Nathaniel
Brent, give these ... Lambeth, July 15,
1618.
[c]   To my loving friend Mr. Nathaniel Brent,
a Daniel Nice ... Croydon, Aug. 10.
1618.
[d]   To my very loaing [sic] friend Mr.
Nathaniel Brent, give these. A Daniel
Nice Ven ... Croydon, Septemb. 9. 1618.
[e]   To my very loving friend Mr. Nathaniel
Brent, give these, at Venice. Al Sig-
nior Daniel Nice ... From Croydon,
September 24. 1618.

Appears in:

> ATTERBURY, Lewis, <u>editor</u>
>   Some letters relating to the History
> of the Council of Trent. London, printed
> for W. Hawes, 1705. pp. 6-11.

Abbot sent Brent to obtain the <u>History of</u>
<u>the Council of Trent</u> (no. 234) and to meet
its authors, Frs. Paolo and Fulgentis.
Brent sent it over from Venice in parts as
it was written and returned to translate it.
Abbot acknowledged the receipt of parts by
referring to them as "Canzoni".

<u>12 SEPT. 1619</u>   <u>TO SECRETARY NAUNTON</u>

71 Archbishop Abbots to Secretarie Nanton, 12
    Septemb. 1619. [Favouring support of the
    Palatinate on religious grounds.]

Appears in:

> CABALA: sive scrinia sacra. [See no. 35.]
>   p. 169.

> SANDERSON, William
>   A compleat history of the lives and
> reigns of Mary Queen of Scotland, and
> James the Sixth King of Scotland ...
> King of Great Britain ... the First, <u>etc.</u>
> London, printed for Moseley [etc.], 1656.
> pp. 481-82. Wing S646.

> COLLIER, Jeremy, <u>the Nonjuror</u>
>   An ecclesiastical history of Great
> Britain. [No. 152.] v. 2, p. 719. (<u>New</u>
> <u>edition</u>, v. 7, pp. 418-19.)

> BIOGRAPHIA BRITANNICA. [See no. 156.]
>   v. 1, pp. 11-12.

Also summarized in the third person in Frankland's <u>Annals</u> (see no. 52), p. 42, where it
is misdated 1612, and in Rushworth's
<u>Collections</u> (see no. 51), p. 12.

9 OCT. 1619   GENERAL DIRECTIONS

72 The archbishop of Canterbury's letter for an uniform manner of prayer before sermon. - Reg. II. Abbot, fol. 181. b.

Appears in:

WILKINS, David, compiler
Concilia. [No. 251.] v. 4, pp. 460-61.

CARDWELL, Edward, D.D.
Documentary annals of the reformed Church of England. [See no. 37.] v. 2, pp. 133-34.

OCT. 1621   TO THE BISHOP OF LINCOLN (JOHN WILLIAMS) AND OTHERS

-- For letters relating to the shooting incident, see nos. 47-50.

13 NOV. 1621   TO JAMES I

73 The archbishop of Canterbury to the King.

Appears in:

GARDINER, Samuel Rawson, editor
The Fortescue papers: consisting chiefly of letters relating to state affairs, collected by John Packer ... Edited from the original MSS. in the possession of the Hon. G.M. Fortescue. London, Camden Society, 1871. (New Series, 1.) pp. 164-65.

AUG.- SEPT. 1622   TO THE BISHOPS

-- For letters concerning preaching articles, see nos. 31-37.

4 SEPT. 1622   TO SIR WILLIAM BOSWELL?

74 [Concerning early Brownist and independent
    churches abroad.]

    Appears in:

        BURRAGE, Champlin
            The early English dissenters. [See
        no. 61.] v. 2, p. 260.

    The original letter is in British Museum
    Add. MS. 6394. ff. 29-30.

20 NOV. 1622   TO SIR THOMAS ROE

75 [On Turkish, Palatinate, and Spanish affairs.]

    Appears in:

        ROE, Sir Thomas
            The negotiations of Sir Thomas Roe.
        [No. 247.] pp. 102-05.

12 AUGUST 1623   TO SIR THOMAS ROE

76 [On Turkish, Palatinate, and Spanish affairs.
    Complains at the ingratitude of his former
    protégé Cristophilus Metrophanes.]

    Appears in:

        ROE, Sir Thomas
            The negotiations of Sir Thomas Roe.
        [No. 247.] pp. 171-72.

23 JUNE 1624   TO SIR THOMAS ROE

77 [On Dutch and Spanish affairs. Further
    complaints about Metrophanes.]

    Appears in:

        ROE, Sir Thomas
            The negotiations of Sir Thomas Roe.
        [No. 247.] pp. 251-53.

28 NOV. 1624   TO SIR THOMAS WENTWORTH, BART.

78 The Archbishop of Canterbury to Sir Thomas
Wentworth, Bart. [On Mr. Greenwood's being
fit for office in Ripon.]

Appears in:

WENTWORTH, Thomas, Earl of Strafford
The Earl of Strafforde's letters and
dispatches ... [Edited] by William
Knowler. London, printed for the editor
by William Bowyer, 1739. v. 1, p. 25.

30 MARCH 1625   TO SIR THOMAS ROE

79 [On various European affairs.   Further
complaints about Metrophanes.   Death of
James I.]

Appears in:

ROE, Sir Thomas
The negotiations of Sir Thomas Roe.
[No. 247.] pp. 371-73.

11 NOV. 1625   TO SIR THOMAS ROE

80 [On various European affairs.]

Appears in:

ROE, Sir Thomas
The negotiations of Sir Thomas Roe.
[No. 247.] pp. 459-61.

1626   TO THE ATTORNEY-GENERAL

81 Archbishop of Canterbury's letter in behalf
of the priests in the Clink, directed to
Master Attorney-General.

Appears in:

[FRANKLAND, Thomas, M.D.]
  The annals of King James and King
Charles the First. [See no. 52.] p. 121.

26 SEPT. 1626   TO THE BISHOPS

-- For the commendation of the subsidy to the
King of Denmark, see nos. 38 and 263.

19 MARCH 1626/27   TO THE ARCHBISHOP OF
ARMAGH (JAMES USHER)

82 [A note recommending Richard Sibbes to be
elected Provost of Trinity College, Dublin.]

Appears in:

        PARR, Richard
          The life of ... James Usher, late Lord
        Arch-Bishop of Armagh... With a
        collection of three hundred letters.
        London, printed for Nathaneal Ranew,
        1686. p. 380. Wing P548.

        USHER, James, Archbishop of Armagh
          The whole works of the Most Rev.
        James Ussher. [See no. 62.] v. 15, p. 375.

2 JUNE 1627   TO THE FELLOWS OF TRINITY
COLLEGE, DUBLIN

83 [A note recommending Bedell for Provost,
Sibbes not having been chosen.]

Appears in:

        USHER, James, Archbishop of Armagh
          The whole works of the Most Rev.
        James Ussher. [See no. 62.] v. 1, p. 87.

1628   TO THE CORPORATION OF GUILDFORD

84 [On further endowments to give employment.]

Appears in:

[RUSSELL, John, editor]
    The history of Guildford. [See no. 66.]
    pp. 16-20.

Ends with note that in 1656 the £100 a year
was distributed in cash to poor tradesmen
and others.

24 MARCH 1629/30   TO THE MAYOR OF GUILDFORD
(R. TERRY)

85   [Letter to the Mayor of Guildford appointing
Jasper Yardley master of the Hospital of the
Blessed Trinity on the death of Abbot's
brother Richard.]

Appears in:

SURREY ARCHAEOLOGICAL COLLECTIONS,
    Guildford, v. 31, 1918, p. 25.

In an article by P.G. Palmer on Yardley.

20 JUNE 1630   TO THE DEAN OF CANTERBURY
(JOHN BOYS)

86   Archbishop Abbot to the Dean of Canterbury.
Concerning the silver-font, formerly used
for the baptism of the King's children.

Appears in:

ARCHAEOLOGIA CANTIANA, Canterbury, v. 42,
    1930, p. 105.

In an article by C.E. Woodruff on some 17th-
century letters and petitions from the
muniments of the Dean and Chapter of Canterbury.

<u>1632</u>   TO THE WARDEN OF ALL SOULS' COLLEGE,
OXFORD (RICHARD ASTLEY)

87 [Seeking to restrain overboisterous be-
    haviour in the college at Christmas.]

    Appears in:

        BURROWS, Montagu
            Worthies of All Souls'. [No. 193.]
        pp. 126-27.

    <u>8 JULY 1633</u>   TO THE PARISHIONERS OF CRAYFORD

88 The archbishop's letter about the minister-
    ing and receiving of the Sacraments in the
    church of Crayford in Kent. - Reg. II.
    Abbot, fol. 143.b.

    Appears in:

        WILKINS, David, <u>compiler</u>
            Concilia. [No. 251.] v. 4, pp. 479-80.

        CARDWELL, Edward, <u>D.D.</u>
            Documentary annals of the reformed
        Church of England. [See no. 37.] v. 2,
        pp. 174-76.

        ADDLESHAW, George William Outram, <u>Dean of
            Chester</u>, <u>and</u> ETCHELLS, Frederick
            The architectural setting of Anglican
        worship, <u>etc.</u> London, Faber and Faber,
        1948. p. 123.

    Abbot comes out against the extreme puritans
    in that he wished communicants to kneel and
    the table to be in the chancel.

D   SERMONS AND SPEECHES

1594-99   SERMONS

For An exposition upon the prophet Jonah, see
nos. 18-20.

6 FEB. 1602   SERMON

89   6 Feb. 1602. At the Temple Churche, Dr.
Abbottes, Deane of [Winchester]. His text, 59 of
Isay, v. 12. [A summary of Abbot's sermon is
given.]

Appears in:

> MANNINGHAM, John
>   Diary of John Manningham ... Edited from
> the original manuscript by John Bruce, etc.
> London, Camden Society, 1868. (Old Series,
> 99.) pp. 126-27.

26 MAY 1608   SERMON

--   For the sermon preached at the Earl of Dorset's
funeral, see nos. 26, 26a.

1612   SERMONS

90   [A summary of Abbot's exhortation to Prince
Henry on his deathbed. - A summary of the sermon
preached by Abbot at the funeral of Prince
Henry.]

Appears in:

> CORNWALLIS, Sir Charles
>   The life and death of our late most incom-
> parable and heroique prince, Henry Prince of
> Wales. A prince (for valour and vertue) fit
> to be imitated in succeeding times. London,

printed by Jn. Dowson for Nat. Butler, 1641.
pp. 64-66, 87-90. Wing C8330.

SCOTT, Sir Walter, Bart., compiler
   A collection of scarce and valuable tracts.
[See no. 41.] v. 3, pp. 242-48.

Cornwallis' book is reprinted in full in the
Somers Tracts volumes.

Cornwallis' book is written in the form of a
letter.

Abbot's sermon was made "with exceeding passion",
on the text of Psalm 82: 6-7; it lasted three
hours.

1621, 1625, 1628   SPEECHES

91   [Speeches in the House of Lords.]

Appears in:

   ENGLAND. Parliament. House of Lords
      Notes of the debates in the House of
   Lords, officially taken by Robert Bowyer and
   Henry Elsing, clerks of the Parliaments, A.D.
   1621, 1625, 1628. Edited from the original
   manuscripts in the Inner Temple library, the
   Bodleian Library and the House of Lords by
   Frances Helen Relf. London, Royal Historical
   Society, 1929. 8°. pp. xxii, 239. (Camden
   Society Publications, 4th Series, 42.)

1621   SPEECHES

92   [Speeches in the House of Lords.]

Appears in:

   ENGLAND. Parliament. House of Lords
      Notes of the debates in the House of
   Lords, officially taken by Henry Elsing,
   clerk of the Parliaments, 1621. Edited from
   the original MS. in the possession of E.G.
   Carew by Samuel Rawson Gardiner. London,

Camden Society, 1870. 8°. pp. ix, 158. (<u>Old Series</u>, 103.)

<u>1621</u>   SPEECHES

93 [Speeches in Parliament of 1621.]

Appears in:

> ENGLAND. <u>Parliament</u>. <u>House of Commons</u>
>   Commons debates, 1621. [Compiled by]
> Wallace Notestein, Frances Helen Relf,
> Hartley Simpson [from twelve journals and
> diaries]. New Haven, Yale University Press:
> London, Oxford University Press, 1935. 8°.
> 7 vols.

The index in v. 1 refers to twelve speeches by
Abbot when the two Houses were meeting jointly,
as well as several references made to him in
debate.

<u>1623</u>   SPEECH

94 [Abbot speaks the opinion and declaration of
the Committee of both Houses favouring three
subsidies and three-fifteenths if the King
broke off both his treaties with Spain.]

Appears in:

> RUSHWORTH, John, <u>M.A.</u>, <u>compiler</u>
>   Historical collections. [See no. 51.] v. 1,
> pp. 134-36.

<u>1623</u>   SPEECH

95 The Archbishop of Canterbury his speech to King
James, at the Council, against the match with
the Infanta of Spain.

Appears in:

> WARE, <u>Sir</u> James, <u>editor</u>
>   The hunting of the Romish fox, and the
> quenching of sectarian firebrands: being a

specimen of Popery and separation. Collection ... out of the memorials of eminent men
both in Church and State, viz. A.B. Cranmer,
A.B. Parker, A.B. Abbot ... And now published
for the publick good by Robert Ware, gent.
Dublin, printed by J. Ray, for Will. Norman,
1683. pp. 164-66. Wing W849.

Not the same as the spurious work no. 124-135.

1624, 1626   SPEECHES

96   [Speeches in the House of Lords.]

Appears in:

ENGLAND. Parliament. House of Lords
Notes of the debates in the House of
Lords, officially taken by Henry Elsing,
clerk of the Parliaments, 1624 and 1626.
Edited from the original MS. in the posses-
sion of E.G. Carew by Samuel Rawson Gardiner.
London, Camden Society, 1879. 8°. pp. [6],
236. (New Series, 24.)

1 JULY 1625   SPEECH

97   [A message from Abbot, who was sick, was read to
the Commons concerning Montagu's Appello
Caesarem.]

Appears in:

ENGLAND. Parliament. House of Commons
Debates in the House of Commons in 1625.
Edited from a MS in the library of Sir
Rainald Knightley, Bart., by Samuel Rawson
Gardiner. London, Camden Society, 1873.
(New Series, 6.) pp. 33-35.

25 APRIL 1628   SPEECH

98   The Lords had a conference [over the Petition of
Right] with the Commons, where the Lord Archbishop of Canterbury spake as followeth.

Appears in:

> [FRANKLAND, Thomas, M.D.]
> The annals of King James and King Charles
> the First. [See no. 52.] pp. 282.

> COBBETT, William, M.P.
> Cobbett's Complete collection of state
> trials. [See no. 46.] v. 3, pp. 165-66.

1631-32   COURT PROCEEDINGS

99 [Various observations, speeches, and judgements
in the Court of High Commission.]

Appears in:

> ENGLAND. Star Chamber
> Reports of cases in the courts of Star
> Chamber and High Commission. Edited by
> Samuel Rawson Gardiner. London, Camden
> Society, 1886. 8°. pp. vii, 328. (New
> Series, 39.)

E   ARCHIEPISCOPAL BUSINESS

I   Visitation articles

The index to Abbot's register shows his metropolitical visitation to have taken place between
1612 and 1616, and I have traced copies of
articles for Canterbury, Lincoln, Norwich, and
Peterborough as well as a factotum set and an
edition of the Bristol articles in Cardwell.
In other visitations Abbot is often accused of
slackness, but I have found printed editions as
listed below and the register also shows visitations in Bristol in 1626, Canterbury in 1629,
and Winchester in 1618 for which no printed
articles seem to survive.

100   METROPOLITICAL: General

[Type orns.] / ARTICLES / To be inquired of, in
the / first Metropoliticall visitation, of the
most / Reuerend Father, GEORGE, by Gods pro- /
uidence, Arch-Bishop of Canterbury, and Primate
of all / England; in, and for the Dioces of
[blank] in / the yeare of our Lord God, 1616.
and in the sixt / yeare of his Graces
Translation. / [device: McK. 283] / LONDON, /
Printed by William Iaggard.

4°. A-B⁴. No pagination or foliation. 16 pages.
    39 lines. r.t. Articles.

Ala, t.p.: Alb, "The tenor of the oath to be
ministred to the Church-wardens and Side-men."
A2a, the Articles. [B.L.] : B4b, blank.

STC 10160.

Seen: O

and in:

> CARDWELL, Edward, D.D.
>   Documentary annals ... New edition.
> Oxford, University Press, 1844. v. 2,
> pp. 167-85.

METROPOLITICAL: Bristol

101 Articles to be inquired of the cathedral church
     of Bristol, in the metropolitical visitation of
     the most reverend father in God, George, by
     God's permission archbishop of Cant. and primate
     of all England, in the year of our Lord God
     MDCXII. - Reg. I. Abbot, fol. 229a.

Appears in:

> WILKINS, David, compiler
>   Concilia. [No. 251.] v. 4, pp. 444-45.

> CARDWELL, Edward, D.D.
>   Documentary annals ... New edition.
> Oxford, University Press, 1844. v. 2,
> pp. 167-85.

METROPOLITICAL: Canterbury

102 [Royal arms, flanked by allegorical figures] /
     ARTICLES / To be inquired of, in the / first
     Metropoliticall visitation, of the most /
     Reuerend Father, GEORGE, by Gods pro- / uidence,
     Arch-Bishop of Canterbury, and Primate of all /
     England; in, and for the Dioces of Canterbury
     in the yeare of / our Lord God, [blank: 1615
     in MS] and in the fifth yeare of his / Graces
     Translation. / [device: McK. 283] / LONDON, /
     Printed by William Iaggard. [Bishop, s is short.]

     4°. A-B^4. No pagination or foliation. 16 pages.
         39 lines. r.t. Articles.

Contents as in no. 100.

OB(910.h.12).

Seen: OB(c.e. and photocopy).

METROPOLITICAL: Lincoln

103   [As no. 102 to] / England; in, and for the
      Dioces of Lincolne, in the yeare of / our Lord
      God, 1613. and in the third yeare of his Graces
      Translation. / [device: McK. 283] / LONDON, /
      Printed by William Iaggard. [Bishop, s is short.]

      4°. A-B^4. No pagination or foliation. 16 pages.
         39 lines. r.t. Articles.

      Contents as in no. 100.

      STC 10237.

      Seen: L.

METROPOLITICAL: Norwich

104   [As no. 102 to] / England; in, and for the
      Dioces of Norwich, in the yeare of / our Lord
      God, 1613. and in the third yeare of his Graces
      Translation. / [device: McK. 283] / LONDON, /
      Printed by William Iaggard. Bishop, s is short.]

      4°. A-B^4. No pagination or foliation. 16 pages.
         39 lines. r.t. Articles.

      Contents as in no. 100.

      STC 10290.

      Seen: CE (lacks B4 and some of A3).

METROPOLITICAL: Peterborough

105   [As no. 102 to] / England; in, and for the
      Dioces of Peterburg, in the yeare of / our Lord
      God,[blank: 1613 in MS] and in the third yeare
      of his / Graces Translation. / [device: McK.
      283] / LONDON, / Printed by William Iaggard.
      [Bishop, s is short.]

      4°. A-B^4. No pagination or foliation. 16 pages.
         39 lines. r.t. Articles.

      Contents as in no. 100.

Ramage   STC 10314after

Seen: LLP.

ORDINARY: Canterbury

106   ARTICLES / To be ministred, en- / quired of,
and answered in the Visi- / tation of the right
Worshipfull IAMES / HVSSEY Doctor of the Ciuill
Law and / Commissarie generall to the most
reuerend Father / in God the Lord Archbishop of
Canter- / bury his Grace within the Citie / and
Diocesse of Cant. / [device: McK. 390] /
¶Imprinted at London / 1619.

4°. A⁴, B². No pagination or foliation. 12
    pages. 39 lines. r.t. Articles.

Ala, t.p.: Alb, "The tenour of the oath to be
mininistred [sic] to the Church-wardens and
Sworne-men.": A2a-B2b, the Articles. [B.L.]

STC 10161.

Seen: L.

Printed by Edward Griffin.

ORDINARY: Canterbury

107   ARTICLES / To be ministred, en- / quired of,
and answered in the Visi- / tation of the right
Worshipfull Sir / NATHANIEL BRENT, Knight /
Doctor of the Civill Law, / Commissary Generall
to the most / Reverend Father in God the Lord /
Archbishop of Canterbury, his / Grace, within
the City / and Diocese of / Canterbury. /
[rule] / [device: McK. 188b] / [rule] / LONDON
/ Printed for RICHARD THRALE at the / Crosse
Keys, by Paules Gate. [1633.]

4°. A⁴, B². No pagination or foliation, 12
    pages. 39 lines. r.t. Articles.

Ala, t.p.: Alb, "The tenour of the oath to be bee
ministred to the Church-wardens and Sworne-
men.": A2a-B2b, the Articles. [B.L.]

STC 10166.

Seen: O.

ORDINARY: Exeter

108   ARTICLES / TO BE ENQVIRED / of in the
      trienniall Visita- / tion of the Diocesse of /
      EXETER / Holden Anno 1627. / By authority of
      the most Reuerend / Father in God, GEORGE Lord
      Archbishop / of CANTERBVRY His Grace, Primate
      / of all ENGLAND and / Metropolitan. / [rule]
      / [woodblock: floral design] / [rule] / ◣
      Imprinted at LONDON / 1627.

      4°. A-B^4, C^4 (-C4). No pagination or foliation.
         22 pages. 38 lines. r.t. Articles.

      Ala, t.p.: Alb, "The oath of the Church-
      wardens and Side-men.": Alb, 1.11, "A monition
      to the minister to read these articles in his
      church.": A2a, the Articles. [B.L.]: C3b, blank.

      STC 10206.

      Seen: DM.

ORDINARY: Lichfield and Coventry

109   ARTICLES / TO BE ENQVIRED / OF, IN THE
      ORDINARIE / Visitation of the most Reuerend
      Father / in God, GEORGE by Gods Providence
      Lord / Arch-Bishop of Canterbury, Primate of
      all England, and Metropolitan: in, and for the
      Cities / and Diocesse of COVENTRY and /
      LICHFIELD, the See / there being / Voyd. /
      Holden in the yeere of our Lord God, 1632. /
      and in the two and twenty yeere of / his Graces
      Tran- / slation / [rule] / [arabesque wood-
      block] / [rule] / Imprinted at London for
      Robert Milbourne 1632.

      4°. A-B^4. No pagination or foliation. 16 pages.
         40 lines. r.t. Articles.

      Ala, t.p.: Alb, "The tenor of the oath to bee
      ministred to the Church-wardens and side-men.":

A2a-B4b, the Articles. [B.L.]

STC 10191.

Seen: CH(m.f. at L).

ORDINARY: Norwich

110 [Royal arms, flanked by allegorical figures]
/ ARTICLES / To be inquired of, in the /
Ordinary Visitation, of the most Reue- / rend
Father, GEORGE, by Gods proui- / dence,
Arch-Bishop of Canterbury, and Primate of all
Eng- / land; in, and for the Dioces of Norwich,
in the yeare of our / Lord God, 1618. and in
the eight yeare of his Gra- / ces
Translation, the Episcopal Sea there / being
voyde / [device: McK. 283] / LONDON, / Printed
by William Iaggard. [Bishop, s is short.]

4°. A⁴, B⁴ (-B4). No pagination or foliation.
14 pages. 39 lines. r.t Articles.

Ala, t.p.: Alb, "The tenor of the oath, to be
ministred to the Church-wardens and Side-men
and Assistants.": A2a-B3b, the Articles. [B.L.]

STC 10291.

Seen: L CE.

II   Miscellaneous

Besides the items listed below, Abbot's commendations to his bishops of royal letters
should be noted. When published during his
lifetime, they are entered as works in part
I, nos 31-38. No. 29 is also in the nature
of an official statement. When, however, both
letter and commendation are published later
from the archbishop's registers or other
sources, they are entered under their subject
in part II, being too brief and formal to rank
properly as works of Abbot's. Nos. 198, 238,
260, and 263 are examples of this class.

<u>1610</u>

111   Negotium consecrationis et dedicationis
       parochialis Sancti Olavi in Silver-street,
       civitat. London. A.D. 1610. [Issued by Abbot.]

       Appears in:

              COLLIER, Jeremy, the Nonjuror
                 An ecclesiastical history of Great
              Britain. [No. 152.] v. 2 p. [2]107. (New
              edition, v. 9, p. 371.)

<u>1612</u>

112   [Notice, drawn up 15 Oct. 1612, to accompany a
       catalogue of Archbishop Bancroft's books which
       were left to the Archbishops of Canterbury to
       form a basis of Lambeth Palace Library.]

       Appears in:

              DUCAREL, Andrew Coltée
                 The history and antiquities of the
              Archiepiscopal Palace of Lambeth, etc.
              London, printed by and for J. Nichols,
              1785. (Bibliotheca topographica
              Britannica, 27.) pp. 48-52.

       and (abridged) in:

              TRANSACTIONS OF THE CAMBRIDGE BIBLIOGRAPH-
                 ICAL SOCIETY, Cambridge, v. 3, 1960,
                 pt. 1. [See no. 200.] pp. 2-3.

<u>1616</u>

113   Consecratio capellae et coemiterii. Ex reg. I.
       Abbot fol. 288.

       Appears in:

              WILKINS, David, compiler
                 Concilia. [No. 251.] v. 4, pp. 555
              [sic for 455] -459.

The proceedings, with a summary of the sermon, at the consecration of a chapel and cemetery at Dulwich, 1 Sept. 1616.

1620/21

114   23 January 1621. Archbishop Abbot admits John Dawson to be a Master Printer (SPD, James I, v. 119, Art. 29, f. 39).

Appears in:

    ARBER, Edward, editor
       A transcript of the Register of the Company of Stationers of London, 1554-1640 A.D. London, privately printed, 1876. v. 3, p. 689.

1624

115   16 November 1624. Archbishop Abbot admits Miles Fletcher to be a Master Printer (SPD, James I, v. 174, f. 68).

Appears in:

    ARBER, Edward, editor
       A transcript of the Register of the Company of Stationers of London. [See no. 114.] v. 3, p. 689.

Both these documents, signed G: Cant., show the continuing authority of the Star Chamber decree of 23 June 1586 concerning orders to print.

1632/33

116   Arch-Bishop Abbot's account of his province for the year 1632. Sent to the king. [Lambeth Jan. 2. 1632.]

Appears in:

LAUD, William, <u>Archbishop of Canterbury</u>
     The history of the troubles and tryal of
... William Laud. [No. 140.] pp. 519-20.

Abbot claimed "there is not in the Church of
England left any inconformable minister."
But there are hints that both Arminians and
separatists are causing trouble.

F   <u>ABBOT'S WILL</u>

    <u>1777</u>

117   The Will of George Abbot.

      Appears in:

          RUSSELL, John, <u>editor</u>
              The life of D̄r George Abbot. [No. 157.]
          pp. 57-71.

    <u>1869</u>

118   "<u>Age Officium Tuum</u>". / [decorated rule] / THE
      WILL / OF GEORGE ABBOT, D.D., / Lord Archbishop
      of Canterbury, / (FROM A.D. 1610. to A.D. 1633.)
      / [rule] / <u>Reprinted from the original at</u>
      <u>Doctors Commons</u>, / <u>in RUSSELL'S LIFE OF ABBOT</u>,
      A.D. 1777. / [rule] / ROBERT SWALES, HIGH ROW,
      DARLINGTON. / 1869.

      8°. [A]^{10}. pp. i-ii, 1-18. 30 lines. r.t.
      Archbishop ABBOT'S Will.

      Edited, with a preface by John Thomas Abbot,
      also with a note on the window from Abbot's
      birthplace now at the editor's home, reprinted
      from the <u>Darlington and Stockton Times</u> of Sept.
      1866.

      There are references in the margin of the BB
      article (no. 156) to an edition of the will by
      Russell, obviously before 1746, but no copy
      has been traced.

   I   Mistaken attribution

   1619

119 [Commemorative poem, no. 154 in Madan's
     numbering.]

     Appears in:

          OXFORD. University
          Academiae Oxoniensis funebria sacra
          aeternae memoriae serenissimae Reginae
          Annae. Oxoniae, excudebant Johannes Lich-
          field et Jacobus Short, 1619. STC 19024;
          Madan i. 1619/7 and ii. 470.

     1623

120 [Commemorative poem, no. 64 in Madan's number-
     ing.]

     Appears in:

          OXFORD. University
          Carolus redux. Oxoniae, excudebant
          Johannes Lichfield et Jacobus Short, 1623.
          STC 19027; Madan i. 1623/5 and ii. 510.

     Madan ii, index, enters both these poems under
     the Archbishop's name, but at this time Abbot
     was only a visitor of All Souls' and had he
     written a poem would have been higher up the
     list. This George Abbot is referred to
     successively as "Coll. Ball. Gen." and "Coll.
     Mert. Soc.", which fits in with the career of
     Abbot's nephew, George, son of Sir Morris,
     Lord Mayor of London.

     1623

121 Look beyond Luther by Richard Bernard (STC
     1956) is ascribed to Abbot in H. Savage's
     Balliofergus.

<u>1632</u> [sic]

122 A letter from the Bishop of Canterbury to the
Bishop of Bath and Wells about Wakes and
revels [dated 4 Oct. 1632].

Appears in:

[FRANKLAND, Thomas, <u>M.D.</u>]
The annals of King James and King
Charles the First. [See no. 52.] p. 437.

The date given is a year too early, Cf. Neal,
<u>The History of the Puritans</u>, v. 2, p. 247,
where it is attributed to Laud and seen as the
harbinger of the renewal of the declaration of
sports a fortnight later. This view is backed
up by W.B. Whitaker, <u>Sunday in Tudor and
Stuart times</u> (London, 1933), p. 127.

<u>1632</u>

123 B., H., <u>and</u> H., I.

The opinion, judgement and determination of
two reverend, learned, and conformable
Divines of the Church of England, concerning
bowing at the name, or naming of Jesus. The
one [H.B.] somtime a member of the Vniuertie
[sic] of Cambridge ... The other [I.H.] some-
time a member of the Vniuersitie of Oxford ...
To the most Reverend, George, Archbishop of
Canterbury, &c... this twofold tractate is in-
scribed and commended.

Printed at Hamburgh, 1632. Reprinted Anno
1634 [by the successors to G. Thorpe at
Amsterdam].

8°. pp. [2], 3-80. STC 14555.

Wood, Watt, BB, and DNB all, with varying
degrees of confidence, put this work in the
Abbot canon. But as the contributions are
initialled and the dedication is to Abbot,
it seems impossible that Abbot could have
been the author; there would have been no need

for anonymity in 1634, after Abbot's death.
The titlepage of the now lost 1632 edition
may have been more ambiguous and have led to
the wrong ascription.

II   Letter or speech to the King

Here are included only editions printed before
1700, after which date publication of the text
was more to illustrate the history of Abbot's
period than to figure in contemporary controversy.   Later works to include the speech, in
as many variant forms as the seventeenth
century knew, include Calderwood (no. 216),
Webster (no. 20), BB (no; 156), and Russell
(no. 157).

The tract does not seem to have been published
in England or in English until after Abbot's
death, for the editor of Mercure françois, in
which a French version appeared in 1624, introduces it and another tract by "Aussi veit on
aussi tost courir de main en main deux
escrits", a phrase re-echoed by Prynne in his
Popish Royall favorite (London, 1643) by "Two
writings [that] ran from hand to hand". SPD,
where it is calendared at James I. CL., 8
Aug., no. 55-57, shows that at court Abbot's
authorship was questioned, and denied, from
the first.   Although doubtless Abbot agreed
with the views expressed, he would not have
written in such terms.   The various texts and
doubts as to whether Abbot wrote or spoke the
words - there was in fact no meeting of the
Privy Council on the day named in the tract -
make more certain the spuriousness of the work.
One curious offshoot of the controversy is
that, guided by an entry in the British Museum
catalogue (now corrected) which assigned the
edition in no. 133 to Sheldon on the strength
of the signature G. Canterbury in 1663, Osmund
Airy in an article "Notes on the reign of
Charles II" in the British quarterly review
(vol. 77, no. 154, 1 April 1883, pp. 317-335)
gave Sheldon for a while an unjustified repu-
tation for intolerance.   See also "A note on
Gilbert Sheldon" by F. M. G. Higham, in

Journal of Ecclesiastical History, v. 14, no. 2, Oct. 1963, pp. 209-12.

Undated   Full version

124   [No titlepage: the contents are described more fully.]

4°. A². pp. 1-4. 21 lines. r.t. None.

A1a, "[row of type orns.] / Arch-Bishop ABBOT'S / SPEECH / TO KING JAMES, / At the Councel Table, / July the 18th. 1623.": A2b, text ends at the foot with "FINIS." Gerould no. 813.

Seen: MiU(photocopy).

Neither date nor imprint, but as the work refers to Archbishop Abbot rather than to the Archbishop of Canterbury it is probably post-1633. Text ends, "And now, Sir, do with me what you please."

Undated   Full version. Dutch

125   DISCOVRS, / Aen sijn Ma^t. van groot Brittangie / IACOBVS / Den Vierden. / Ghedaen door d'Arts-Bisschop van / Cantelbury. / In't Iaeronses Heeren, 1623.

4°. A². No pagination or foliation. 4 pages. 33 lines. r.t. None.

A1a, t.p.: A1b, blank: A2a-A2b, text. [B.L.]

Seen: CE.

1624   Full version. French

126   [No heading]

Appears in:

Le MERCURE françois, etc. A Paris. Chez

Iean & Estienne Richer, 1624. tom. 9.
pp. 497-99.

1642   Shortened version

127   [Within a border of type orns.] THE /
SVPPLICATION / OF ALL THE PAPISTS OF ENGLAND,
/ TO / KING JAMES, / At his first comming to
the Crowne, / For a Tolleration of their
Religion, / Wherein (with much impudence) they
professe / and protest themselves, to be the
onely obedient one's / unto the Soveraigne
Princes (under whom they live) / out of
conscience to avoid sin: When not long after
they / fell upon that un-exampled piece of
villany / (The Gun-pouder Treason.) / [rule]
/ Whereunto is added, A letter sent from
Bishop Abbot / Archbishop of Canterbury, to
the King: against / Toleration of the Popish
Religion. / [rule] / Published for the
observation of all good Protestants. / [rule]
/ LONDON, / Printed by E. Griffin, 1642.

4°. A⁴. pp. [2], 1-6. 32 lines. r.t. None.

A1a, t.p.: A1b, blank: A2a, the petition:
A4a-b, Abbot's letter.

Wing S6189   Thomason E.151(19).

Seen: L.   Not seen: CT O.

The part between "detestable" and "that dread-
ful consequence" is omitted. Ends "And now,
Sir, do with me what You please."

1656   Full version

128   [No heading.]

Appears in:

PRYNNE, William
    Hidden workes of darkenes brought to
publike light, etc. London: printed by
Thomas Brudenell for Michael Sparke senior,
1645. pp. 39-40. Wing P3973.

<u>1653</u>   <u>Full version</u>

129   [No heading.]

Appears in:

    WILSON, Arthur
      The history of Great Britain, <u>etc.</u>
    London, printed for Richard Lowndes, 1653.
    p. 236. Wing W2888.

Ends "And now, Sir, do with me what you
please."

<u>1654</u>   <u>Full version</u>

130   The Archbishop of York [<u>sic</u>] to King James.

Appears in:

    CABALA: sive scrinia sacra. [See no. 35.]
      pp. 13-14.

Ends "And now Sir, Do with me what you please."

<u>1655</u>   <u>Full version</u>

131   [No heading.]

Appears in:

    FULLER, Thomas, <u>D.D.</u>, <u>Prebendary of</u>
      <u>Salisbury</u>
      The Church-history of Britain. [No.
    142.] p. 106. (<u>Later edition</u>, v. 5,
    pp. 547-49.)

Ends "And now, Sir, doe with me what you
please." The later edition is annotated and
has variant readings from O (Tanner MS
lxxiii).

<u>1659</u>   Full version

132   [No heading.]

Appears in:

>   RUSHWORTH, John, <u>M.A.</u>, <u>compiler</u>
>   Historical collections. [See no. 51]
>   p. 85.

Ends "Now, Sir, do what you please with me."
There are two interesting changes coming
possibly from setting from dictation: "a
large" and "a liberty" in earlier editions
change to "a charge and" and "ability" -
and still make sense in their places.

<u>1663</u>   Shortened version

133   [Within a double rule] FAIR-WARNING: / [seven
short rules] / OR, / XXV. REASONS / Against
<u>Toleration</u> and <u>Indulgence</u> of / Popery; WITH
THE / Arch-Bishop of <u>Canterbury</u>'s / LETTER /
TO THE / KING, / AND / All the Bishops of
<u>Irelands</u> Protestation / to the <u>Parliament</u> to
the same purpose. / With an / Answer to the
Roman-Catholicks reasons / FOR / <u>INDVLGENCE.</u>
/ [six short rules] / ALSO THE / **Excellent
Reasons of the Honourable** / HOUSE of COMMONS /
Against INDULGENCE; / **with Historical
Observations thereupon.** [six short rules] /
<u>**London**</u>, **Printed for S.U.N.T.F.S., 1663.**

4°. $\underline{A}^4$, $A-B^4$, $D-F^4$. pp. [9], 2-39, [1].
33 lines. r.t. None.

<u>A</u>1a, t.p.: <u>A</u>1b, blank: <u>A</u>2a, "To the Kings
most excellent Majesty": <u>A</u>3a, Irish protesta-
tion: $\underline{A}4a$, Bishop of Worcester's letter: A1a,
Twenty five reasons. [signed: Richard Baxter,
Catholique.]: D4a, 1.14, "An answer to the
Roman Catholiques Reasons for Indulgence.":
F1a, Reasons of the House of Commons: F4b,
blank.

Wing B1263.

Seen: L.

The part between "detestable" and "Besides, this toleration" is omitted. Ends "And now, sir, doe with me what you please." The old reading "a liberty" is used. By using the signature G. Canterbury for the letter was the publisher leading his readers to believe that Sheldon was the author?

1683   Full version

134   [No heading.]

Appears in:

> WARE, Sir James, editor
>   The hunting of the Romish fox. [See no. 95.] pp. 169-72.

Apparently copied from Rushworth, no. 132.

1688/89   Full version

135   [No titlepage: the contents are described more fully.]

4°. A⁴. pp. 1-5, [1], 7-8. Lines vary.
     r.t. None.

Ala, "The Declaration of the Nobility, Gen- / try, and Commonalty at the Rendezvous at Notting- / ham, Nov. 22. 1688." [B.L.] : A3b, blank: A4a, "His Grace the / Arch-Bishop of Canterburys / ADDRESS, to his MAJESTY, / For the Suppression of Monasteries, Fry- / ries, Nunneries, and other Popish Semi- / naries, or allowing any General Tollera- / tion to the Roman Catholicks of England." : A4b, text ends, "Printed in the year 1689."

Wing D718.

Seen: L.

Apparently copied from Rushworth, no. 132.

PART II

WORKS ABOUT GEORGE ABBOT

A   GENERAL

I   Fasti

136   LE NEVE, John
      Fasti Ecclesiae Anglicanae; or, an essay
      towards deducing a regular succession of all
      the principal dignitaries in each cathedral,
      collegiate church or chapel ... To which is
      added ... the heads ... of each college ...
      in either of our Universities.
      In the Savoy, printed by J. Nutt, and sold
      by Henry Clements, [etc.] , 1716.
      2°. pp. [2] , iii-xii, 1-535, [5] .

      Basic work for dates of election, etc. A re-
      vised edition, edited by Sir T. Duffus Hardy,
      was published by O.U.P. in 1854.

II   Contemporary

137   [BIRCH, Thomas, D.D., compiler]
      The court and times of James the first;
      illustrated by authentic and confidential
      letters, from various publick and private
      collections. Edited, with an introduction
      and notes, by the author of "Memoirs of Sophia
      Dorothea", etc. [i.e. Robert Folkestone
      Williams].
      London, Henry Colburn, 1848.
      8°. 2 vols.

      References to Abbot are said to occur, but
      there is no index.

138   [BIRCH, Thomas, D.D., compiler]
      The court and times of Charles the first;
      illustrated by authentic and confidential
      letters, from various publick and private
      collections... Edited, with an introduction

and notes, by the author of "Memoirs of Sophia
Dorothea," etc. [i.e. R. F. Williams].
    London, Henry Colburn, 1848.
    8°. 2 vols.

References to Abbot are said to occur, but
there is no index.

139 CHAMBERLAIN, John, <u>Commissioner for the repair
     of St. Paul's</u>
        The letters of John Chamberlain. Edited
     with an introduction by Norman Egbert McClure.
        Philadelphia, American Philosophical
     Society, 1939.
        8°. 2 vols. (<u>Memoirs</u>, 12.)

140 LAUD, William, <u>Archbishop of Canterbury</u>
        The history of the troubles and tryal of
     the Most Reverend Father in God, and Blessed
     Martyr, William Laud wrote by himself... To
     which is prefixed the diary of his own life,
     faithfully and entirely published from the
     original copy, and subjoined a supplement to
     the preceding history, etc. [with accounts of
     his Province].
        London: printed for Ri. Chiswell, 1695.
        2°. pp. [20], 1-616, [2]. Wing L586.

p. 3: Claims Abbot incited Ellesmere against
him in 1610.

p. 8: Laud says King could not believe Abbot
wrote "Of the Visitation [sic] of the
Church" in 1624.

pp. 517-18: "Instructions sent from the King
to the Arch-Bishop Abbot, in the year 1629."
These were inspired by Laud.

See also no. 116.

Later edition:
    The works of the Most Reverend Father in
God, William Laud. Vol. III. Devotions, diary
and history. **Edited by James Bliss. Oxford,
Parker, 1853.**

141   YONGE, Walter
        Diary of Walter Yonge, Justice of the Peace
      and M.P. for Honiton, written at Colyton and
      Axminster, co. Devon, from 1604 to 1628.
      Edited by George Roberts.
        London, Camden Society, 1868.
        8°. pp. xxxii, 124. (Old Series, 41.)

      pp. 42-44, 106-09: Accident and sequestration.

III   After 1633

142   FULLER, Thomas, <u>D.D.</u>, <u>Prebendary of Salisbury</u>
        The Church-history of Britain; from the
      birth of Jesus Christ, untill the year
      M.DC.XLVIII.
        London, printed for Iohn Williams, 1655.
        2°. 13 pt. in 1 vol. Wing F2416.

      Book 10: Fuller claims that Abbot's seques-
      tration was for homicide, but denies that
      Forde was a centre of separatist activity
      while Abbot was there.

      Abbot is discussed in vols. 5-6 of J.S.
      Brewer's edition (Oxford, 1845). See also no.
      131 for an edition of the spurious letter.

143   FULLER, Thomas, <u>D.D.</u>, <u>Prebendary of Salisbury</u>
        The history of the worthies of England.
      Endeavoured by Thomas Fuller, D.D.
        London, printed by J.F., W.L. and W.G.,
      1662.
        2°. 4 parts. Wing F2440.

      p. 83: "George Abbot". One of the better-known
      unfavourable portraits.

      An "alphabetical index" was published in 1744.

Later edition (abridged):
    The worthies of England ... Edited with an
introduction and notes by John Freeman.
London, Allen and Unwin, 1952.

144   LLOYD, David, <u>Canon of St. Asaph</u>
    The statesmen and favourites of England
since the Reformation, their prudence and
policies, successes and miscarriages, advance-
ments and fall, <u>etc.</u> [1509-1649].
    London, printed by J.C. for Samuel Speed,
1665.
    8°. pp. [14], 1-623, [1]. Wing L2648.

pp. 522-25: "Observations on the life of Archbishop Abbot." From the second edition of 1670
this work took the title <u>State worthies</u>, by
which it has since been known.

145   HEYLIN, Peter
    Cyprianus Anglicus: or the history of the
life and death of the most reverend and re-
nowned prelate William [Laud] ... Containing
also the ecclesiastical history of the three
kingdoms ... from his first rising till his
death.
    London: printed for A. Seile, 1668.
    2°. 3 pt. in 1 vol. Wing H1699.

<u>Passim</u> in pt.1. There is no index to this
edition, and the second edition (Dublin,
1719), with an index, is recommended. Very
antagonistic.

146   AUBREY, John
    "Brief lives", chiefly of contemporaries,
set down by John Aubrey, between the years
1669 & 1696. Edited from the author's MSS. by
Andrew Clark.
    Oxford, Clarendon Press, 1898.
    8°. 2 vols.

v. 1, p. 24: "George Abbot". On his birth and
temper only. Aubrey's MSS were used by Wood
(no. 147).

Later edition:
    Aubrey's Brief lives. Edited from the
original manuscripts and with an introduction
by Oliver Lawson Dick. **London, Secker &
Warburg, 1949.**

pp. 3-4: "George Abbot" - with a brief note by
the editor. Portrait.

Aubrey's "life" of Abbot, consisting mostly of
the prognostications of his birth, appeared
originally in the only work Aubrey published
himself, the Miscellanies of 1696. This has
been slightly augmented from the MS sources.

147 [WOOD, Anthony à]
    Athenae Oxonienses: an exact history of all
the writers and bishops who have had their
education in the most ancient and famous University of Oxford, from ... 1500 to ... 1690
... To whom are added the Fasti, or annals, of
the said university for the same time.
    London, printed for Tho. Bennet, 1691-92.
Wing$_o$W3382-83.
    2°. 2 vols.

v. 1, cols. 499-500, 629: Contains earliest
useful list of Abbot's works.

Fasti give the dates of his proceeding to
degrees and offices.

Later edition:
    - ------ By A. a Wood. A new edition with
additions and a continuation by Philip Bliss.
London, Rivington [etc.] , 1813-15.

Most of the additions are from Le Neve (no.
154), who owed much of his material to the
first edition of Wood.

148 HACKET, John, Bishop of Lichfield and Coventry
    Scrinia reserata: a memorial offer'd to the
great deservings of John Williams, who some
time held the places of Ld Keeper of the Great
Seal of England, Ld Bishop of Lincoln, and Ld
Archbishop of York: containing a series of the

most remarkable occurrences and transactions
of his life, in relation both to Church and
State.
     In the Savoy: printed by Edw. Jones, for
Samuel Lowndes, 1693.
     2°. 2 pt. in 1 vol. Wing H171.

Passim, but no index.

149 WELWOOD, James
     Memoirs of the most material transactions
in England, for the last hundred years, pre-
ceding the Revolution in 1688.
     London, printed for Tim. Goodwin, 1700.
     8°. pp. [24], 1-405, [9]. Wing W1306.

L has 2nd ed., 1700. LW copy seen. pp. 37-41.

   IV Eighteenth Century

150 HYDE, Edward, Earl of Clarendon
     The history of the rebellion and civil wars
in England begun in the year 1641, etc.
     Oxford, printed at the Theater, 1702-04.
     2°. 3 vols.

v. 1, pp. 68-69: Very hostile. Abbot "considered Christian religion no otherwise than
as it abhorred and reviled Popery." Short,
but notorious and the basis of most later
hostile assessments of Abbot. Refuted in
Russell (no. 157) by Arthur Onslow.

Later edition:
     ------ Re-edited from a fresh collation of
the original MS. in the Bodleian Library, with
... notes, by W. Dunn Macray. Oxford, Clarendon Press, 1888. 6 vols.

151 KENNET, White, Bishop of Peterborough
     The history and life of King Charles I ...
All new writ by a learned and impartial hand.

Appears in:

[HUGHES, John, poet, compiler and editor]
A complete history of England: with the lives of all the kings and queens thereof from the earliest account of time to the death of ... William III, etc. London, printed for Brab. Aylmer [etc.] , 1706. v. 3, pt. 1.

Comparatively sympathetic to Abbot.

152 COLLIER, Jeremy, the Nonjuror
An ecclesiastical history of Great Britain, chiefly of England, from the first planting of Christianity, to the end of the reign of King Charles the Second ... Collected ... by Jeremy Collier.
London, printed for Samuel Keele and Benjamin Tooke [etc.] , 1708-14. 2°. 2 vols.

v. 2, pp. 704-55, covers Abbot's archiepiscopate. For original letters, etc., see nos. 35n, 56, 71, 111.

Later edition:
------ A new edition, with a life of the author ... by Thomas Lathbury, etc. London, Straker, 1852. 9 vols.

vols. 7-9 cover Abbot's archiepiscopate.

153 AUBREY, John
The natural history and antiquities of the county of Surrey. Begun in the year 1673, and continued to the present time.
London, printed for E. Curll, 1718-19. 8°. 5 vols.

v. 3, pp. 280-91: In the chapter on Guildford a propos Abbot's Hospital, the Royal Grammar School, and the Church of Holy Trinity, Abbot's birth, foundation, and monument are described. Aubrey adds a spiteful comment against Abbot's spreading of Puritanism and quotes Clarendon at length.

154   LE NEVE, John
         The lives and characters, deaths, burials,
      and epitaphs, works of piety, charity, and
      other munificent benefactions of all the
      Protestant bishops of the Church of England
      since the Reformation, etc.
         London: printed by W. Bowyer for William
      and John Innys, 1720.
         8°. pp. [16], 1-268, [4].

      pp. 89-116: "George Abbot". Factual and well-
      documented record, but not entirely accurate.
      Notes consecrations made by Abbot. The work
      did not reach beyond v. 1, covering arch-
      bishops only.

155   NEAL, Daniel
         The history of the Puritans or Protestant
      Non-Conformists ... with an account of their
      principles, their attempts for a further re-
      formation in the Church, their sufferings,
      and the lives and characters of their
      principal divines.
         London, printed for Richard Hett, 1732-38.
         8°. 4 vols.

      v. 2, pp. 242-44: Favourable character.

      Later editions:
         ------ A new edition ... reprinted from the
      text of Dr. Toulmin's ... revised, corrected
      and enlarged. London, Baynes, 1822. 5 vols.

      v. 2, pp. 209-12: Character, including
      editorial note on sources.

156   [OLDYS, William]
               Abbot ⟨George⟩.

         Appears in:

            **BIOGRAPHIA BRITANNICA: or, the lives of
               the most eminent persons who have
               flourished in Great Britain and Ireland
               from the earliest ages down to the
               present times. Collected from the best
               authorities ... and digested in the**

manner of Mr. Bayle's Historical and
critical dictionary. London, printed
for W. Innys [etc.], 1747. v. 1, pp.
3-17.

Wholly favourable; copious footnotes and bibliographical references; source of information
concerning most of the works written before
1747.

The article is signed G., which in the preface
to the second edition of 1778 is ascribed to
William Oldys.

For Russell's edition of this article, see no.
157.

For original works by Abbot in this article,
see nos. 63, 71. The spurious letter as in
no. 132 is printed also.

157 RUSSELL, John, editor
      The life of Dr. George Abbot, Lord Arch-
bishop of Canterbury, reprinted with some
additions and corrections from the Biographia
Britannica; with his character, by the Rt.
Hon. Arthur Onslow, late Speaker of the House
of Commons; a description of the Hospital,
which he erected and endowed in his native
town of Guildford in Surrey; correct copies
of the charter and statutes of the same, his
will, &c. To which are added the lives of
his two brothers, Dr. Robert Abbot, Lord
Bishop of Salisbury; and Sir Morris Abbot,
Knt. Lord-Mayor of the City of London.
      Guildford; printed for and sold by
J. Russell, bookseller, 1777.
      8°. pp. [4], 1-54, [3], 52-55*, [4],
58-156, [2], 157-58. Plates of Abbot, Sir
Nicholas Kempe, and Abbot's Hospital, and in
one copy at GuPL of Abbot's birthplace and
Guildford Royal Grammar School. The latter
copy also has an additional leaf after p. 83
showing the sources of the hospital's rents.

p. 1, "The life of Archbishop Abbot.": p. 54
+ 1, "Character of Archbishop Abbot.": p. 57
"The will of George Abbot." [no. 117]: p. 73,

letter [no. 66]: p. 77, "A description of the
Hospital at Guildford.": p. 85, "The charter":
p. 101, "The oath of the King's supremacy":
p. 103, "The Statutes of the Hospital.": p.
143, "A list of the master.": p. 147, "The
life of Bishop Abbot.": p. 157, "The life of
Sir Morris Abbot."

The article reprinted from BB is shorn of its
marginal references, and the main authorities
have been listed on the third preliminary page.

GuPL also has an interleaved edition with MS
notes and additions and the beginnings of
amending the text of the statutes of the
hospital; this is known as "Russell notebook,
5." The hand appears to be that of John
Russell's son Thomas (1748-1822), rector of
Clandon. GuPL also has a folio volume known as
the "Abbot book," which contains, roughly, the
text of the book in MS and other extracts, the
BB article being extracted from the printed
book. For further particulars of the bibliographical sources in GuPL, see pages xi, xx.

Original material by Abbot in both this work
and BB is listed in part I under the latter
only; see nos. 63 and 71.

   V   Nineteenth Century

 158   WRANGHAM, Francis
        The British Plutarch, containing the lives
of the most eminent divines ... of Great
Britain and Ireland from the accession of
Henry VIII to the present time. A new edition,
etc.
        London, J. Mawnan, 1816.
        8°. 6 vols.

v. 2, pp. 519-42: "George Abbot, Archbishop of
Canterbury, 1562-1633." Ample footnotes,
favourable, quotes opinions, including Onslow's
in full (see also no. 157).

159 LODGE, Edmund
       Portraits of illustrious personages of
     Great Britain. Engraved from authentic
     pictures ... With biographical and historical
     memoires of their lives and actions.
         London, Lackington, Longman [etc.] , 1821-34.
         2°. 3 vols.

     v. 1, pp. 1-4, of text: "George Abbot,
     Archbishop of Canterbury."

160 HOOK, Walter Farquhar, <u>Dean of Chichester</u>
       An ecclesiastical biography, containing the
     lives of ancient fathers and modern divines,
     forming a brief history of the Church in every
     age.
         London, F. & J. Riving**ton** [etc.] , 1845-52.
         8°. 12 vols.

     v. 1, pp. 7-30: "Abbot, George". A forerunner
     to Hook's lives of archbishops (no. 166), and
     still more antagonistic to Abbot.

161 WEBSTER, Grace
       The life of George Abbot, D.D., Archbishop
     of Canterbury.

     Appears in:

         ABBOT, George, <u>Archbishop of Canterbury</u>
         An exposition upon the Prophet Jonah,
         by George Abbot ... A new edition by
         Grace Webster. To which is added a life
         of the author. [No. 20.] v. 1, pp.
         v-xxiv.

     Quotes several extracts and letters without
     identifying them. See no. 20 for details.

162 McCLURE, Alexander Wilson
       The translators revived; a biographical
     memoir of the authors of the English version
     of the Holy Bible.
         New York, Scribner, 1853.
         12°. pp. 250.

pp. 152-61: "George Abbot." Favourable, but
nothing original. Says shooting accident was
in 1619 and that this was ground for sequestration. Probably the book is more useful for
more obscure translators.

163   SPEDDING, James
        The letters and life of Francis Bacon, in-
cluding all his occasional works ... Newly
collected and set forth ... by James Spedding.
        London, Longmans, 1861-74.
        8°. 7 vols. (vols. 8-14 of The Works of
Francis Bacon ... Collected and edited by
James Spedding, 1857-74.)

vols. 4-7, especially v. 5. For letter from
Abbot, see no. 64.

164   ABBOT, John Thomas
        An apology for Dr. George Abbot, Lord Arch-
bishop of Canterbury, as touching some
strictures on his memory: with his Character
by the Right Honourable Arthur Onslow and a
brief account of his life.
        Darlington, Swales: Guildford, Andrews:
London, Coleman, 1863.
        8°. 19 p., family tree.

No copy at L. GuA copy seen.

An answer to a few relatively mild strictures
in The Churchman's family magazine, v. 1, no.
2, Feb. 1863, pp. 159-60.

165   GARDINER, Samuel Rawson
        History of England from the accession of
James I. to the disgrace of Chief Justice Coke.
        London, Hurst and Blackett, 1863.
        8°. 2 vols.

        Prince Charles and the Spanish marriage:
1617-1623: a chapter of English history, etc.
        London, Hurst and Blackett, 1869.
        8°. 2 vols.

A history of England under the Duke of
Buckingham and Charles I., 1624-1628.
London, Longmans, Green, 1875.
8°. 2 vols.

The personal government of Charles I: a
history of England from the assassination of
the Duke of Buckingham to the declaration of
the judges on ship-money.
London, Longmans, Green, 1877.
8°. 2 vols.

Later edition (with two further volumes):

History of England from the accession of
James I. to the outbreak of the Civil War,
1603-1642. London, Longmans, Green, 1883-84.
10 vols.

Passim in vols. 2-7; see index in v. 10. This
and the DNB are the most detailed accounts
before P.A. Welsby's. Gardiner tries to be
fair to Abbot and, indeed, is more gentle than
the DNB.

166   HOOK, Walter Farquhar, Dean of Chichester
      Lives of the archbishops of Canterbury.
      London, Bentley, 1870-75.
      8°. 12 vols.

v. 10, chaps. 30-32, also chap. 29, and v. 11,
chaps. 33-34. An unsympathetic Anglo-Catholic
viewpoint.

167   PATTISON, Mark
      Isaac Casaubon, 1559-1614.
      London, Longmans, Green, 1875.
      8°. pp. 543.

The second edition (Oxford, 1892), edited by
H. Nettleship, has an index. Abbot was very
friendly with Casaubon on the latter's visit
to England 1610-14.

168   LEE, Sir Sidney
          Abbot, George.

Appears in:

      STEPHEN, Sir Leslie, K.C.B., editor
          Dictionary of national biography.
      London, Smith, Elder, 1885. v. 1,
      pp. 5-20.

Well documented and with a summary bibliography. Emphasizes Abbot's morose personality
at the expense of his conscientiousness. An
uninspired account written by a professional
biographer.

169   FOX, Arthur William
          A book of bachelors ... with illustrations.
      Westminster, Constable, 1899.
      8°. pp. xvi, 449.

      pp. 157-202: "The archbishop: George Abbot."
      With portrait and references. Sympathetic
      and attacks Heylin (no. 145).

  VI   Twentieth Century

170   FRERE, Walter Howard, Bishop of Truro
          The English Church in the reigns of
      Elizabeth and James I, 1558-1625.
          London & New York, Macmillan, 1904.
          8°. pp. xiii, 413. (A history of the
      English Church, 5.)

      pp. 366-89: "The days of Abbot." - an Anglo-
      Catholic approach.

171   McKILLIAM, Annie E.
          A chronicle of the Archbishops of
      Canterbury.
          London, Clarke, 1913.
          8°. pp. 472.

      pp. 333-38: "73. - George Abbot, 1611 to 1633."
      Nothing original; practically impartial.

172   MATHEW, David, <u>Archbishop of Apamea</u>
        The Jacobean age.
        London, Longmans Green, 1938.
        8°. pp. 354.

      <u>Passim</u>, especially pp. 94-113: Emphasizes
      Abbot's charity and kindness as well as his
      ambition.

173   TREVOR-ROPER, Hugh Redwald
        Archbishop Laud, 1573-1645.
        London, Macmillan, 1940.
        8°. pp. ix, 464.

      Unsympathetic to Laud, but also to Abbot;
      makes pertinent points and is probably the
      first treatment of Abbot (albeit as a sub-
      sidiary character) not affected by local or
      theological affiliations. Second edition
      1962.

174   HIGHAM, Florence May Grier
        Lancelot Andrewes
        London, S.C.M. Press, 1952
        8°. pp. 128.

      pp. 58ff, 100ff: Admits Andrewes might have
      been too yielding to be archbishop, but Abbot
      was "not in the rich flowering of Anglican
      faith and worship."

175   KAUTZ, Arthur Philip
        The Jacobean episcopate and its legacy: a
      study of the episcopacy in Canterbury and
      York during the reign of King James I, <u>etc</u>.
        [Minneapolis, University of Minnesota],
      1952.
        8°. pp. [2], 249.

      Generally available only on microfilm (Univer-
      sity Microfilms Publication, 4893). Submitted
      for the degree of Ph.D. in the University of
      Minnesota. No copy at L; LU microfilm copy
      seen.

References to Abbot <u>passim</u>, but no index.
Adequate bibliography.

176   SODEN, Geoffrey Ingle
        Godfrey Goodman, Bishop of Gloucester,
      1583-1656.
        London, S.P.C.K., 1953.
        8°. pp. xiii, 511.

Relations of Abbot with Goodman.

177   TREVOR-ROPER, Hugh Redwald
        King James and his bishops. A study of
      "worldly, courtly, talented place-hunters",
      who betrayed the principles of the English
      Church.

Appears in:

        HISTORY TODAY, London, v. 5, no. 9, Sept.
          1955, pp. 571-81.

Portrait of Abbot: Abbot described as a "skilful courtier, indifferent, negligent,
secular".

178   ROGAN, John
        King James's bishops.

Appears in:

        **THE DURHAM UNIVERSITY JOURNAL, Durham,
          v. 48, no. 3, June 1956, pp. 93-99.**

179   WILLSON, David Harris
        King James VI. and I.
        London, Cape, 1956.
        8°. pp. 480.

180   BOWEN, Catherine Shober Drinker
        The lion and the throne: the life and times
      of Sir Edward Coke, 1552-1634.
        London, Hamish Hamilton, 1957.
        8°. pp. xiv, 531.

Especially useful for Abbot's relations with
the Court of High Commission and his legal
position with regard to the shooting accident.

181 McELWEE, William Lloyd
        The wisest fool in Christendom: the reign
     of King James I and VI.
        London, Faber and Faber, 1958.
        8°. pp. 296.

182 WELSBY, Paul Antony
        Lancelot Andrewes, 1555-1626.
        London, S.P.C.K., 1958.
        8°. pp. xiv, 298.

     Stresses Abbot's involvements in the court.
     Excellent bibliography and indexes.

183 WELSBY, Paul Antony
        George Abbot: the unwanted archbishop,
     1562-1633.
        London, S.P.C.K., 1962.
        8°. pp. xiii, 174.

     Standard biography. Portraits, also plates of
     Lambeth Palace, University College, Abbot's
     Hospital and tomb. Bibliography.

B   FAMILY

184   ABBOT, Family of
         [Genealogical table.]

      Appears in:

            SURREY ARCHAEOLOGICAL COLLECTIONS,
               Guildford, v. 2, 1864, $a3b-4a.

      In "Genealogical and heraldic memoranda
      relating to the County of Surrey" published
      as a supplement to the Collections.

185   **ABBOTT, Lemuel Abijah**
         Descendents of George Abbott of Rowley,
      Mass... with brief notes on many others of
      the name, original settlers in the United
      States.
         Printed privately, 1906.
         8°. 2 vols.

      v. 1, pp. xix-lxxiii: "The Guildford Abbotts."
      Reprints DNB articles with comments, pedigree,
      portraits, arms, pictures of Abbot's Hospital.

C   ACADEMIC LIFE

See also works by Abbot, nos. 1-22, 30, 112, and letters, nos. 82, 83, 87.

I Oxford

186 BODLEY, <u>Sir</u> Thomas
     Reliquiae Bodleianae... Containing ... a
collection of letters to Dr. James, &c, <u>etc.</u>
London: printed for John Hartley, 170$\overline{3}$.
8°. pp. [16], 1-383, [1].

Letters 87, 126, 135, 146, 155, 164, 198, and
225 concern Abbot.

Later edition of the letters:

     Letters of Sir Thomas Bodley to Thomas
James... Edited with an introduction by G.W.
Wheeler.
     Oxford, Clarendon Press, 1920.
4°. pp. xliii, 249.

In this edition letters have been assigned
dates and arranged in correct order with an
index.

187 MALLET, Charles Edward
     A history of the University of Oxford.
London, Methuen, 1924-27.
8°. 3 vols.

188 CURTIS, Mark Hubert
     Oxford and Cambridge in transition, 1558-
1642: an essay on changing relations between
the English universities and English society.
     Oxford, Clarendon Press, 1959.
     pp. vii, 314.

pp. 120, 223, 236-39: Little new, mostly
credited to the DNB.

189 SACKVILLE, Thomas, <u>Earl of Dorset</u>
        [A letter from Dorset, Chancellor, to
     Abbot, Vice-Chancellor, following the King's
     visit to Oxford.]

     Appears in:

        WAKE, <u>Sir</u> Isaac
           Rex Platonicus: sive, de potentissimi
        principis Jacobi Britanniarum Regis, ad
        illustrissimam Academiam Oxoniensem,
        adventu, Aug. 27. Anno 1605. Narratis ab
        Isaaco Wake, Publico Academiae ejusdem
        Oratore, <u>etc</u>. Oxoniae, excudebat Iosephus
        Barnesius, 1607. $"R3"a-b [<u>sic</u> for S3 .]
        STC 24939; Madan i. 1607/10.

190 DAVIS, Henry William Carless
        Balliol College.
        London, Robinson, 1899.
        8°. pp. x, 237. (<u>University of Oxford</u>
     <u>college histories</u>.)

     pp. 90-127 <u>passim</u>: Abbot as Fellow of Balliol.

191 CARR, William, M.A.
        University College.
        London, Robinson, 1902.
        8°. pp. xiv, 242. (<u>University of Oxford</u>
     <u>college histories</u>.)

     pp. 92-98: Abbot as Master of University
     College.

192 MACLEANE, Douglas
        A history of Pembroke College at Oxford,
     anciently Broadgates Hall, <u>etc</u>.
        Oxford, Oxford Historical Society, 1897.
        8°. pp. xvi, 4, 544. (<u>Publication</u>, 33.)

Deals with Abbot's part in the foundation of
Pembroke College.   Facsimiles of Abbot's
signature.

193   BURROWS, Montagu
         Worthies of All Souls': four centuries of
English history illustrated from the College
archives.
         London, Macmillan, 1874.
         8°. pp. xv, 452.

pp. 125-138: Abbot as Visitor of All Souls'
College. Includes some brief extracts from the
Tanner MSS. Abbot's injunctions of 1626 en-
abled the Commissioners of 1852 to report
favourably on All Souls'. Also an account of
Abbot's support of Mocket (q.v. no. 207). For
letter by Abbot, see no. 87.

194   ROBERTSON, Sir Charles Grant
         All Souls' College.
         London, Robinson, 1899.
         8°. pp. xvi, 234. (University of Oxford
college histories.)

pp. 97-107: Abbot as Visitor.

II   Inner Temple

195   BAX, Alfred Ridley
         Members of the Inner Temple, 1547-1660 ...
connected with the county of Surrey.

Appears in:

         SURREY ARCHAEOLOGICAL COLLECTIONS, Guild-
              ford, v. 14, 1899, pp. 19-41.

p. 25: Abbot admitted to Inner Temple,
Nov. 1610.

III   Bible

196   ENGLAND. Miscellaneous Public Documents
       An order set down by King James the First
for translating of the Bible.

Appears in:

       BURNET, Gilbert, Bishop of Salisbury
       The history of the reformation of the
       Church of England. The Second Part: of
       the progress made in it till the settle-
       ment of it in the beginning of Q. Eliza-
       beth's reign. London, printed by T.H. for
       Richard Chiswell, 1681. pp. 366-68.
       Wing B5798.

       Later edition:

       ----- By Nicholas Pocock. Oxford,
       Clarendon Press, 1865, v. 5, pp. 559-62.

       CARDWELL, Edward, D.D.
       Documentary annals of the reformed
       Church of England. [See no. 37.] v. 2,
       pp. 106-12.

For an entry for the text of the Authorized
Version and a list of Abbot's colleagues in
the work of translation, see no. 30.

197   BUTTERWORTH, Charles Collier
       The literary lineage of the King James
Bible, 1340-1611.
       Philadelphia, University of Pennsylvania
Press, 1941.
       8°. pp. xi, 394.

pp. 206-43: "The King James Bible." General
background without mention of Abbot except in
passing. With a bibliography of other books
on the Authorized Version.

IV   Chelsea College

198   JAMES I
      A briefe declaration of the reasons that
moved King James of blessed memory, and the
state, to erect a colledge of Divines, and
other learned men at Chelsey. Together with
a copy of his majesties letters in favouring
the same. And an addition of some motives
forcible to excite good Christians zeale to
a voluntary and liberall contribution.
      London, printed by E.P. for Nicholas
Browne, 1645.
      4°. pp. [1], 2-8. Wing B4564.

Includes a letter of 5 May 1616 from the King
to Abbot for sending to the bishops. Abbot's
commendatory letter is printed on p. 4.

V   Library

199   COX-JOHNSON, Ann
      Lambeth Palace Library, 1610-64.

Appears in:

      **TRANSACTIONS OF THE CAMBRIDGE BIBLIO-
         GRAPHICAL SOCIETY, Cambridge, v. 2,
         1955, pt. 2, pp. 105-26.**

Abbot wrote in the preface of the MS list of
Bancroft's books. A catalogue of Abbot's 2667
books was made in MS, c. 1633. [Some of
Abbot's books are also in the library of St.
Andrew's University. I am indebted to Mr.
Ramage of Durham University Library for this
information. Abbot left or presented others,
including a Jesuit Bible of 1632, to the
library of his old school, Guildford Royal
Grammar School.]

200   JAMES, Montague Rhodes
             The history of Lambeth Palace Library.

Appears in:

**TRANSACTIONS OF THE CAMBRIDGE BIBLIO-
    GRAPHICAL SOCIETY, Cambridge, v. 3,
    1960, pt. 1, pp. 1-31.**

Published from a MS which James intended as
an epilogue to a catalogue of the library's
later MSS. Includes Abbot's note to the
catalogue of Bancroft's books (see no. 112)
and references to Abbot's bequest.

D   THEOLOGY

This section has much common ground with the
following section, "Court and Politics". For
the distinction I have attempted to make, see
the Introduction.

I   General

For general theological writings by Abbot, see
nos. 1, 2, 18, 19, 20, 26, 26a, 30, 68. For
documents relating to Abbot's administrative
work, see nos. 100-116, 246, 251.

201   ADDISON, James Thayer
        Early Anglican thought, 1559-1667.

Appears in:

   HISTORICAL MAGAZINE OF THE PROTESTANT
      EPISCOPAL CHURCH, New Brunswick, N.J.,
      v. 22, no. 3, Sept. 1953, pp. 24-369.

Abbot is not among the 18 representative
divines whose works are chosen to illustrate
the course of thought, but this article pro-
vides an excellent background to the
theological position of his day.

202   DAVIES, Godfrey
        Arminian versus Puritan in England, ca.
1620-1640.

Appears in:

   HUNTINGTON LIBRARY BULLETIN, Cambridge,
      Mass., no. 5, April 1934, pp. 157-79.

General background of the religious position
of the times but no mention of Abbot.

203 JORDAN, William Kitchener
      The development of religious toleration in
England from the accession of James I to the
convention of the Long Parliament, 1603-1640.
      London, Allen and Unwin, 1936.
      8°. pp. 542.

II The maintenance of the Anglican Settlement

For relevant material by or attributed to
Abbot, see nos   29, 31-37, 55-55c, 62, 72,
78, 88, 123.

204 HIGHAM, Florence May Grier
      Catholic and reformed. A study of the
Anglican Church, 1559-1662.
      London, S.P.C.K., 1962.
      8°. pp. viii, 358.

1603

205 BARLOW, William, Bishop of Rochester and
      of Lincoln
      The summe and substance of the conference,
which, it pleased His Excellent Maiestie to
have with the Lords Bishops, and other of his
clergie ... at Hampton Court, Ianuary 14.
1603 ... Whereunto are added, some copies,
(scattered abroad,) unsavory and untrue.
      London, printed by Iohn Windet, for
Mathew Law, 1604.
      4°. pp. [9], 2-103, [9]. STC 1456.

Strype in his Life and acts of John Whitgift
(London, 1717) says that this was not published until after it was compared with the
notes of others present at the conference,
including Abbot. Abbot is not recorded as
saying anything.

Reprinted in:

      CARDWELL, Edward, D.D.
      A history of conferences and other pro-
ceedings connected with the revision of

the Book of Common Prayer from the year
1558 to the year 1690. Oxford, University
Press, 1840. pp. 167-212.

1606

206   OVERALL, John, Bishop of Lichfield and
      Coventry and of Norwich
      Bishop Overall's Convocation-Book, MDCVI.
Concerning the government of God's Catholick
Church, and the Kingdoms of the whole world.
London, printed for Walter Kettilby, 1690.
4°. pp.[8], 1-338, [2]. Wing 0607.

Examined by Abbot in 1606 and considered too
Catholic, but published by Archbishop Sancroft before his sequestration in 1690. In
three books, transcribed from Overall's MSS
of the Convocations of 1603-10.

Reprinted:

   The Convocation Book of MDCVI. Commonly
called Bishop Overall's Convocation Book, con-
cerning the government of God's Catholic
Church and kingdoms of the whole world.
Oxford, Parker, 1844. (Library of Anglo-
Catholic theology, 28.)

Includes a preface with a letter from James I
to Abbot deploring Convocation's entering into
such a theory of politics. The text is
corrected from the errata of the 1690 edition
with notes and readings.

1616

207   [MOCKET, Richard]
      Doctrina, et politia ecclesiae Anglicanae,
a beatissimae memoriae Princibus Edovardo
Sexto, Regina Elizabetha Stabiliae, et a
religiosissimo, & potentissimo Monarcho Iacobo
... Quibus eiusdem Ecclesiae apologia
praefigitur pro sua discessione in utraque a
gravissimis Romanae Ecclesiae corruptelis,
tyrannide, idolatria, erroribus, & quod ad
Concilium Tridentinum non accesserit, etc.

Londini, apud Ioannem Billium, 1616.
4°. pp. [16] , 1-350, [2]. STC **17991**.

An amalgamation of seven other books. This
edition was burnt in spite of Abbot's protest
since the King considered it to be too much in
favour of the primacy and against some of the
39 Articles. Mocket was Warden of All Souls'
and a close friend of Abbot, who was Visitor
to the College. There was a second edition in
1617, **of which Abbot's own copy is at Washington C.**

1622

208   ENGLAND.   Miscellaneous Public Documents
      King James' instructions to the Archbishop
of Canterbury concerning orders to be observed
by Bishops in their dioceses. [Dated 1622.]

Appears in:

CABALA. [See no. 35.]   **pp. 187-88.**

Includes a demand for an annual report.

209   ADDLESHAW, George William Outram, Dean of
      Chester
      The High Church tradition.   A study of
liturgical thought of the seventeenth century.
London, Faber and Faber, 1941.
8°.   pp. 204.

pp. 141-42: Abbot decides in 1622 that white
veils should be worn for churchings.

1624

210   MONTAGU, Richard, Bishop of Chichester and
      of Norwich
      A Gagg for the new Gospell? No: a new gagg
for An old Goose.   Who would needes undertake
to stop all Protestants mouths for ever, with
276 places out of their owne English Bibles.
Or an answere to a late Abridger of Controuer-
sies and Belyar of the Protestants Doctrine
[i.e. Matthew Kellison]. Published by Authority

London: printed by Thomas Snodham for
Matthew Lownes and William Barret, 1624.
4°. pp. [40], 1-328. STC 18038.

Attacked mildly by Abbot but decision reversed
by James I. Answers "errors" imputed to
Protestants, showing they do not believe these
(though many would). For the sequel to this
work, Appello Caesarem, see section E, no.
264.

1625

211 MASON, Francis, Archdeacon of Norfolk
     Vindicae Ecclesiae Anglicanae; sive de
legitimo eiusdem ministerio, id est, de epis-
coporum successione, consecratione,
electione, & confirmatione... Editio secunda,
priori Anglicanâ longè auctior, & emendatior
... Opus ex idiomate Anglicano traductum, &
locupletatum ab ipso Authore Franc. Masono.
     Londini, impressum per Felicem Kyngstonum,
1625.
     2°. pp. [22], 1-680. STC 17598.

Sir Nathanial Brent in his preface explains
how he and Abbot sponsored the Latin translation of this work, first published (in
English) in 1613, but since "in tenebris".

p. 393: Chart of consecrators of Abbot and
their consecrators, etc. Contents show what
is added from the first English edition.

1630

212 PRYNNE, William
     Anti-Arminianism, or the Church of Englands
old antithesis to new Arminianisme... The
second edition much enlarged.
     [London,] Imprinted 1630.
     4°. pp. [56], 1-280, [20]. STC 20458.

The appendix concerns bowing at the name of
Jesus. There is also a list of writers (including Abbot) who have "given publike
testimony against Pelagians, Papists,

Arminians, etc." The dedication is to all
the archbishops and bishops, but is more
admonitory than flattering.

213   WIDDOWES, Giles
        The lawless kneelesse schismaticall
Puritan. Or a confutation of the author of
an appendix, concerning bowing at the name
of Jesus.
        Printed at Oxford for the Author, 1631.
8°. pp. [4], 1-90, [1]. STC 25593.

214   PRYNNE, William
        Lames Giles his haultings. Or, a briefe
survey of Giles Widdowes his confutation of
an appendix, concerning bowing at the name of
Jesus, etc.
        [London] Imprinted for Giles Widdowes,
1630 [sic].
     4°. 2 pt. STC 20465.

        1631

215   PAGE, William, Fellow of All Souls' College
        A treatise or iustification of bowing at
the name of Iesus. By way of answers to an
appendix against it. Together with an examination of such considerable reasons as are
made by Mr. Prinne in reply to Mr. Widdowes
concerning the same argument.
        Oxford, printed by John Lichfield, 1631.
     4°. pp. [16], 1-206. STC 19096; Madan i.
1631/2.

An answer to Prynne's tracts (nos. 212, 214).
Abbot tried to suppress this work. His
position is shown in his letter to the
parishioners of Crayford (no. 88). A tract
on the subject published in Hamburg in 1632
has also been incorrectly ascribed to him
(see no. 123).

III   Relations with other churches (except Roman
      Catholic)

      For letters by Abbot on this subject, see nos.
      56-59, 61, 63, 69, 74.

      Scotland

216   CALDERWOOD, David
         The true history of the Church of Scotland,
      from the beginning of the Reformation, unto
      the end of the Reigne of King James V., etc.
      [Edinburgh?,] 1678.
      2°. pp. [8], 1-839, [1]. Wing C279.

      Later edition:

         **The history of the Kirk of Scotland. Edited
      from the original manuscript ... by the Rev.
      Thomas Thomson. Edinburgh, The Wodrow Society,
      1842-49. 8 vols.**

      vols. 5, 7, 8 passim: Includes Abbot's
      spurious speech. The 1678 edition has no index.

217   [LANG, David, editor]
         Original letters relating to ecclesiastical
      affairs of Scotland, chiefly written by, or
      addressed to H.M. King James the Sixth after
      his accession to the English throne.
      Edinburgh, [Bannatyne Club,] 1851.
      4°. 2 vols. (Publication, 92.)

      Includes one letter by Abbot (see no. 68).

      Protestants, outside Scotland

218   SCHICKLER, Fernand de, Baron
         Les églises du réfuge en Angleterre.
      Paris, Librairie Fischbacher, 1892.
      8°. 3 vols.

219   A SVRVEY of the Booke of Common Prayer...
      Reviewed, corected [sic], and augmented, etc.
         [London,] 1610.
         8°. A-P⁸. STC 16451.

      Warns that Puritans will be persecuted no less
      if Abbot becomes archbishop.

220   SYKES, Norman, Dean of Winchester
         Old priest and new presbyter. [Episcopacy
      and Presbyterianism since the Reformation
      with special relation to the Churches of
      England and Scotland.]
         Cambridge, University Press, 1956.
         8°. pp. viii, 266.

      pp. 90-92: Abbot installs De Laune and
      Calandrinus in parishes, although they had not
      received episcopal ordination.

   IV   Controversy with Grotius, Vorstius,
           Lubbertus, etc.

221   LUBBERTUS, Sibrandus
         Brief D. Sibrandi Lubberti, professors tot
      Franiker: gheschreven aenden Eervveerdichten
      Aertsbisschop van Cantelberch, Primat van
      Enghelandt... Wt het Latyn int Duytsch ghe-
      trouvvelijck overgheset.
         Tot Delf, by Bryn Harmannssz Schinekel,
      1613.
         4°. pp. [2]-128.

      The letter was sent to Abbot with the book
      Apostasio sanctorum.

      The King was shocked that Lubbertus should
      claim that Church of England beliefs were
      expressed in the book, and he had Vorstius'
      books burnt.

222   GROOT, Hugo de
         Ordinum Hollandise ac Westfrisiae pietas.
      Ab Improbissimis Multorum Calumniis, simul'
      que à nupera Sibrandi Lubberti Epistola, quam

ad Reverendissimum Archiepiscopum Cantuarien-
sem scripsit, vindicata per Hugonem Grotium
Eorundem Ordinum Fisci Advocatum, etc.
     Excudit Lugduni Batavorum Iohannes Patius,
Iuratus & Ordinarius Academiae Typographus,
1613.
     4°. pp. [9], 2-126, [2].

Also translated into Dutch, 1613.

223 HARRISON, Archibald Harold Walter
     Vorstius and James I: a theological inter-
lude in diplomacy.

Appears in:

   **THE LONDON QUARTERLY REVIEW, London, v. 142
     (fifth series, v. 28), no. 2, Oct. 1924,
     pp. 198-210.**

224 HARRISON, Archibald Harold Walter
     The beginnings of Arminianism to the Synod
of Dort ... Thesis approved for the degree of
Doctor of Divinity in the University of London.
London, University of London Press, 1926.
     8°. pp. viii, 408.

225 HARRISON, Arthur Harold Walter
     Arminianism.
     London, Duckworth, 1937.
     8°. pp. 246. (Studies in Theology.)

226 WITTE, Horst
     Die Ansichten Jakobs I. von England über
Kirche und Staat, mit besonderer Berücksich-
tigung der religiösen Toleranz.
     Berlin, Ebering, 1940.
     8°. pp. 167. (Historische Studien, 362.)

   V Pelagians

227   BRADWARDINE, Thomas, <u>Archbishop of</u>
        <u>Canterbury</u>
          De causa Dei contra Pelagium, et de vir-
        tute causarum, ad suos Mertonenses, libri
        tres. Iussu Reverendiss. Georgii Abbot
        Cantuariensis Archiepiscopi; Opera et studio
        d^1. Henrici Savilii ... Ex scriptis codicibus
        nunc primum editi.
          Londini, ex officina Nortoniana, apud
        Ionanem Billium, 1618.
          2^0. ¶1, a-b^6, c^4, A-Dddd^6. STC 3534.

        Sponsored by Abbot and Savile.

228   An HISTORICALL narration of the judgement of
        some most learned and Godly English bishops,
        holy martyrs, and others ... concerning Gods
        election and the merit of Christ his death, &c.
          London, printed by B.A. and T.F. for
        Samuel Nealand, 1631.
          4^0. pp. [8], 1-108. STC 4.

        A MS note by Thomason in the edition of 1645
        (Wing A804) states that this work was "called
        Inn: by George Abbot Bp. of Canterbury because
        in it was contained divers dangerous opinions
        both of Pelagianisme & Arminianisme it was
        Licend by Edw: Martine then Chaplen to Wm
        Laude ... and [Laud was] condemed by the House
        of Commons now sitting to loose his head for
        Crimen Lese Maiestat... This shall serve for
        þe Instruction of the reder that shall see
        this new title printed. 10 decemb. 1644.

        The 1645 edition has additional titlepage as
        before but stating "Formerly suppressed by the
        Bishop of Canterbury, but now Published for
        the comfort of all Gods people. London:
        Printed for Rebecca Nealand. 1645." Thomason
        wrote over "Bishop of Canterbury" the words
        "Geo. Abbott; not Wm Laude", which caused the
        British Museum catalogue of 1831 to list this
        work under Abbot. The Bodleian has it under
        Abbot (George), M.P. for Guildford (nephew of
        Abp. Abbot) but notes "The authorship of G.
        Abbot must be considered doubtful, the
        authority for it cannot be found." The preface

is signed "J.A. of Ailward." The printers in
1631 were Bernard Alsop and Thomas Fawcett.

VI   Attack on the Roman Catholic Church

For relevant material by or attributed to
Abbot, see nos. 23-25, 39, 65, 70, 81, 124-31.

General

229 HAVRAN, Martin Joseph
        The Catholics in Caroline England.
     Stanford, Stanford University Press;
     London, Oxford University Press, 1962.
     8°. pp. ix, 208.

230 LEYS, Mary Dorothy Rose
        Catholics in England, 1559-1829. A social
     history.
        London, Longmans, 1961.
     8°. pp. x, 220.

1600

231 GERARD, John, Jesuit
        The condition of Catholics under James I.
     Father Gerard's Narrative of the Gunpowder
     Plot. Edited, with his life, by John Morris.
        London, Longmans, Green, 1871.
     8°. pp. cclxii, 344.

pp. clvi-clvii: The fugitive Gerard,
incognito, meets and debates with Abbot.

Later edition:

     John Gerard. The autobiography of an Eliza-
bethan. Translated ... by Philip Caraman, etc.
London, Longmans, Green. 1951.

pp. 170-71: Gerard's meeting with Abbot.

A second edition was published in 1956.

232   HILL, Edmund Thomas, <u>D.D.</u>
      A quartron of reasons of Catholike
religion, with as many briefe reasons of
refusall: collected, & composed, by Thomas
Hill Doctour of Divinity.
      Printed at Antwerpe, with Priniledge [<u>sic</u>],
1600.
      8°. pp. [14], 1-159, [1], 160-87. STC 13470.

The twenty-five reasons stated. - errata. -
"Coppy of a letter sent... to theyr friend
... beyond the Seas for cause of religion." -
the reasons set out [as quoted by Abbot] - a
copy of another letter. - "An aunswere to the
letter afore going."

      <u>1603</u>

233   DILLINGHAM, Francis
      A quartron of reasons, composed by Doctor
Hill, vnquartered, and prooued a quartron of
follies.
      Printed by Iohn Legat, Printer to the
Vniuersitie of Cambridge, 1603.
      4°. pp. [6], 1-204, [2]. STC 6889.

The first answer to Hill, anticipating
Abbot's by a year.

      <u>1620</u>

234   SARPI, Pietro [<u>aliter</u> PAOLO, <u>Servita</u>]
      The historie of the Councel of Trent.
Containing eight bookes. In which ... are de-
clared many notable occurrences...Written in
Italian by Pietro Soave Polano [i.e. P.
Sarpi], and faithfully translated into English,
by Nathaniel Brent.
      London, printed by Robert Barker and
John Bill, 1620.
      2°. pp. [12], 1-825, [17]. STC 21761.

This and subsequent English editions are dedicated to Abbot by Brent. See also no. 70.

1621

235   KING, Henry, Bishop of Chichester
          A sermon preached at Pauls Crosse, the 25.
    of November. 1621. Upon occasion of that
    false and scandalous Report (lately Printed)
    touching the supposed apostasie of John King,
    late Lord Bishop of London. By Henry King, his
    Eldest Sonne. Whereunto is annexed the Exam-
    ination, and Answere of Thomas Preston, P.
    taken before my Lords Grace of Canterbury,
    touching this Scandall. Published by authority.
          At London, imprinted by Felix Kyngston for
    William Barret, 1621.
          4°. A-L^4, M^3. STC 14949.

    M1a-M3a: "The examination of Thomas Preston,
    taken before the Lord Archbishop of Canter-
    bury, at Lambeth, Decemb. 20. 1621."

    Preston said that John King was not converted
    to Roman Catholicism by his agency.

    1622

236   GAGE, George, the elder
          Mr. George Gage's letter from Rome to the
    Archbishop of Canterbury. [Dated 6 March
    1622/23. With descriptive commentary.]

    Appears in:

          WARE, Sir James, editor
             The hunting of the Romish fox. [See no.
          95.] pp. 166-69.

    See also no. 237 below.

237   REVILL, Philippa and STEER, Francis William
          George Gage I. and George Gage II.

    Appears in:

          BULLETIN OF THE INSTITUTE OF HISTORICAL
             RESEARCH, London, v. 31, no. 2, Nov.
          1958, pp. 141-58.

George Gage the elder was involved in the
diplomacy of the Spanish marriage and wrote
to Abbot from Rome against Roman Catholics.
The appendix gives his letter of 6 March
1622/23, as in Ware (no. 236).

1625

238   CHARLES I
      The king's letter to the archbishop of
Canterbury touching recusants. - Reg. II.
Abbot, fol. 211. a. [dated by the King
Windsor the 15th day of December. In the
form of an introduction and commendatory
letter from Abbot to the other bishops].

Appears in:

      CARDWELL, Edward, D.D.
      Documentary annals of the reformed
Church of England. [See no. 37.] v. 2,
pp. 155-58.

      WILKINS, David, compiler
      Concilia. [No. 251.] v. 4, p. 470.

1630

239   [ANDERTON, Lawrence]
      The conuerted Iew. Or certaine dialogues
between Micheas a learned Iew and others,
touching divers points of religion, contro-
uerted betweene the Catholicks and Protestants. Written by M. Iohn Clare a Catholicke
Priest, of the Society of Iesus [i.e. L.
Anderton], etc.
      [Douai?] 1630.
      4°. 3 pt. STC 5351.

pt. 2, pp. 121-55: "An appendix wherein is
taken a short view, containing a full
answere, of a pamphlet entitled A Treatise of
the perpetuall visibility and succession of
the true Church in all ages." Here, and elsewhere in the work "Clare" ascribes the authorship to Abbot's chaplain, Dr. Featley, who
entered the pamphlet in the Register and was

possibly the "enthusiastic supporter" who
originated the publication. STC ascribes
the tract to Roger Anderton, Halkett and
Laing to Lawrence Anderton.

E   COURT AND POLITICS

    I   General

        For reports of Parliamentary and court pro-
        ceedings in which Abbot took part, see nos.
        91-99. For Abbot's comments to Sir Thomas Roe
        on current events, see nos. 75-77, 79, 80.

240   AKRIGG, George Philip Vernon
            Jacobean pageant: or, the court of King
        James I., etc.
            London, Hamish Hamilton, 1962.
            8°. pp. xi, 431.

241   ALLEN, John William
            English political thought, 1603-1660.
        Vol. 1, 1603-1644.
            London, Methuen, 1938.
            8°. pp. x, 525.

        Brief comment only on Abbot, but chapters on
        political significance of Montagu, Mainwaring,
        and Sibthorpe.

242   DAVIES, Godfrey
            English political sermons, 1603-1640.

        Appears in:

            HUNTINGTON LIBRARY QUARTERLY, San Marino,
                v. 3, no. 1, Oct. 1939, pp. 1-22.

        Shows powers of censorship given to arch-
        bishops to prevent sedition in times when
        many sermons were printed and there were few
        other printed sources of news.

243   ENGLAND. <u>Parliament</u>. <u>House of Lords</u>
          Journals of the House of Lords. Vols. 2-4
       [1578-1624].
       ------ General index to [vols. 1-10] of the
       journals of the House of Lords, 1509-1649.
          [London, by authority of the House of
       Lords], 1836.
          2°. 3 vols.

244   HEAD, Ronald Edwin
          Royal supremecy and the trials of bishops,
       1558-1725.
          London, S.P.C.K. for the Church Historical
       Society, 1962.
          8°. pp. x, 150.

       pp. 37-58 deal with the shooting accident and
       the Sibthorpe affair.

245   HILL, John Edward Christopher
          Economic problems of the Church from Arch-
       bishop Whitgift to the Long Parliament.
          Oxford, Clarendon Press, 1956.
          8°. pp. xiv, 367.

       On the whole unfavourable. Abbot's failure
       to maintain discipline is criticized.

246   NICHOLS, John, <u>F.S.A., printer</u>
          The progresses, processions and magnifi-
       cent festivities of King James the First, his
       royal consort, family and court. Collected
       from original manuscripts ... illustrated with
       notes ... by John Nichols.
          London, J.B. Nichols, 1828.
          4°. 4 vols.

       vols. 1-3 <u>passim</u>: See Index III. The fullest
       account of Abbot's relations with the court.

247   ROE, <u>Sir</u> Thomas
          The negotiations of Sir Thomas Roe in his
       embassy to the Ottoman Porte, from the year
       1621 to 1628, <u>etc</u>. [Edited by Samuel Richard-
       son.]

London: printed by Samuel Richardson, 1740.
2°. pp. [2], iii-xviii, [1], ii-lxii, [2],
1-828.

With eleven letters from Roe to Abbot, mainly
on observations of religious customs, and five
letters from Abbot to Roe. (See nos. 75-77,
79, 80.)

248   RYMER, Thomas, <u>antiquary</u>, <u>compiler</u>
        Foedera, conventiones, literae, et cujus-
cunque generis acta publica, inter reges
Angliae, et alios ... ab ineunte saeculo duo-
decimo ... ad nostra usque tempora ...
Accurante Roberto Sanderson. [Continued by
him from Rymer.]
        Londini: per W. Churchill, 1704-32.
        2°. 22 vols.

vols. 17-19: These give the texts of various
commissions, etc., upon which Abbot served
from 1617 to 1633. See contents pages of the
various volumes.

249   TURNER, Edward Raymond
        The Privy Council of England in the seven-
teenth and eighteenth centuries, 1603-1784.
        Baltimore, Johns Hopkins Press, 1927-28.
        8°. 2 vols.

250   VIRGINIA COMPANY OF LONDON
        The records of the Virginia Company of
London... Edited ... by Susan Myra Kingsbury,
<u>etc.</u>
        Washington, Government Printing Office,
1906-35.
        4°. 4 vols.

251   WILKINS, David, <u>compiler</u>
        Concilia Magnae Britanniae et Hiberniae
... A.D. CCCCXLVI ad MDCCXVII, <u>etc.</u>
        Londini, sumptibus R. Gosling [etc.], 1737.
        2°. 4 vols.

v. 4, pp. 444-80, concerns Abbot's primacy.
For original documents, etc., see nos. 36, 38,
72, 101, 113, 238, 260, 263, 267.

Includes a letter of 1604 from the King to
Abbot wondering why the people were less keen
to help the Dutch then than in Elizabeth's
reign; the mandate for Abbot and others to
consecrate three Scots bishops; King Charles's
letter of 17 July 1632 to Abbot touching the
patronage of benefices.

252   WILLSON, David Harris
        Summoning and dissolving Parliament,
      1603-25.

      Appears in:

        THE AMERICAN HISTORICAL REVIEW, New York
          and London, v. 45, no. 2, Jan. 1940,
          pp. 279-300.

II   Specific events

      For Abbot's preface to Hart's report on
      Sprot's trial, see nos. 27-28. For a letter
      of 1612 from Abbot to the King telling of
      treasonable practices of the Spanish ambas-
      sador, see no. 60. For material by Abbot, or
      ascribed to him, on the Essex divorce case,
      his shooting accident, and his sequestration,
      see nos. 40-54. For a letter of 1614 from
      Abbot to the bishops on raising a loan, see
      no. 64. For a letter of 1615 from Abbot to
      Buckingham, see no. 67. For a letter of 1619
      from Abbot to Haunton favouring support of
      the Palatine, see no. 71. For Abbot's part
      at the deathbed of Prince Henry, see no. 90.
      For speeches by Abbot in Parliament on
      specific events, see nos. 94, 95, 97, 98.

      1611   High Commission

253   USHER, Ronald Greene
          The rise and fall of the High Commission.
          Oxford, Clarendon Press, 1913.
          8°. pp. 380.

          pp. 212-21: Abbot defends High Commission at
          the time of Coke's final attack on it.
          May 1611.

      1613   Essex divorce case

254   McELWEE, William Lloyd
          The murder of Sir Thomas Overbury.
          London, Faber, 1952.
          8°. pp. 280.

          Deals with Abbot's part in Essex divorce case;
          has portrait of Abbot. For other relevant
          material, see nos. 40-46.

255   PARRY, Sir Edward Abbott
          The Overbury mystery: a chronicle of fact
      and drama of the law.
          London, T. Fisher Unwin, 1925.
          8°. pp. 328.

      1614   Parliament

256   MOIR, Thomas Lane
          The Addled Parliament of 1614.
          Oxford, Clarendon Press, 1958.
          8°. pp. x, 212.

          For Abbot's part in this Parliament.

      1615   Introduction of Buckingham

257   ERLANGER, Philippe
          L'énigme du monde: George Villiers, duc de
      Buckingham.
          [Paris], Gallimard, 1951.
          8°. pp. 350. (Leurs Figures.)

      Translated:
          George Villiers, Duke of Buckingham.

Translated by Lionel Smith-Gordon.
London, Hodder and Stoughton, 1953.
8°. pp. 278.

1618   Declaration of Sports

258   ENGLAND.   Miscellaneous Public Documents
The Kings Maiesties Declaration to his
subiects, concerning lawfull sports to be
vsed.
London. Printed by Bonham Norton, and
Iohn Bill, 1618.
4°. pp. [2], 1-9, [1].

Reprinted in:

ARBER, Edward, compiler
An English garner. [No. 54] v. 4,
pp. 511-16. (Later edition: Social England
illustrated. Introduction by Andrew Lang,
pp. 309-14.)

259   HART, Arthur Tindal
The country clergy in Elizabethan & Stuart
times, 1558-1660.
London, Phoenix House, 1958.
8°. pp. 180.

p. 73: Abbot investigates the suspension of
vicar of Elsfield, Worcs., who denounced the
Declaration of Sports. (Other references are
of no original importance.)

1621   Collection

260   ENGLAND.   Privy Council
The council's letter to the archbishop of
Canterbury for a collection for the French
protestants. Reg II Abbot fol. 194b ...
From Croydon the 28. of September, M.Dc.XXI.

Appears in:

WILKINS, David, compiler
Concilia. [No. 251] v. 4, pp. 461-62.

In the form of Abbot's letter accompanying
the despatch of this letter to his bishops.

1621   Shooting accident

261   [Various documents relating to the accident.]

Appears in:

    SPELMAN, Sir Henry
      Reliquiae Spelmannianae. [See no. 47.]
    pp. 111-26.

Fuller details are given under no. 47. Later
editions are at nos. 48-50.

262   WILLIAMS, John, Archbishop of York
    John Williams, Bishop of Lincoln, to the
Lord Admiral [Buckingham], upon the accident
of Archbishop Abbot killing a man by a shot
from a cross-bow. His own affairs respecting
the Great Seal. < MS. Harl. 7000.. art. 30.
Orig. > [Dated 27 July 1621.]

Appears in:

    ELLIS, Sir Henry, editor
      Original letters illustrative of English
    history ... Third Series, London, Bentley,
    1846. v. 4, pp. 183-87.

With a footnote including Chalmers' account
of the accident and his opinion as to whether
Abbot should lose his estate.

1621/22   Subsidy

263   JAMES I
    The king's letter to the archbishop of
Cant. and the bishop of Lincoln about a
voluntary contribution from the clergy. -
Reg. Abbot, II, fol. 195b. [Dated 24 Jan.
1621/22. Commendation dated 21 Jan. 1621/22.]

Appears in:

WILKINS, David, compiler
Concilia. [No. 251.] v. 4, p. 464.

CARDWELL, Edward, D.D.
Documentary annals of the reformed
Church of England. [See no. 37.] v. 2,
pp. 141-45.

1625   Suppression of Appello Caesarem

264   MONTAGU, Richard, Bishop of Chichester
and of Norwich
Appello Caesarem. A iust appeale from two
vniust informers.
London, printed for Matthew Lownes, 1625.
4°. pp. [24], 1-320, [2]. STC 18030.

For A gagg for the new Gospell? No., see
no. 210.

265   ENGLAND.   Proclamations
By the King. A proclamation, for the sup-
pressing of a booke, intituled, Appello
Caesarem, or, An appeale to Caesar ... given
... the seuenteenth day of Ianuary, etc.
Imprinted at London by Bonham Norton, and
Iohn Bill, 1628 [i.e. 1628/29].
Vertical broadside. STC 8912.

1626   Coronation of Charles I

266   WORDSWORTH, Christopher, Fellow of Peterhouse
The manner of the coronation of King
Charles the First of England at Westminster,
2 Feb., 1626. Edited for the Henry Bradshaw
Liturgical Text Society by Chr. Wordsworth.
London, [The Society,] 1892.
8°. pp. lxviii, 147. (Publication, 2.)

Transcriptions of various MSS relevant to the
coronation service, which was drawn up by a
committee headed by Abbot, although Laud had
a background influence.

1626-27   Subsidy to King of Denmark
           and sequestration

267   CHARLES I
       Instructions directed from the Kings Most
       Excellent Maiestie, vnto all the Bishops of
       this kingdome, and fit to be put in execution,
       agreeable to the necessitie of the Time.
       London, printed by Bonham Norton and
       Iohn Bill, 1626.
       4°. A-B⁴. STC 9247.

The letter is in the form of Abbot's commendation of the King's letter of 21 Sept. 1626
[no. 38]. But the letter was really drawn up
by Laud and led to Sibthorpe's exhortatory
sermon (no. 268).

Also appears in:

    WILKINS, David, compiler
       Concilia. [No. 251.] v. 4, pp. 471-73.

    CARDWELL, Edward, D.D.
       Documentary annals of the reformed
    Church of England. [See no. 37.] v. 2,
    pp. 158-64.

268   SIBTHORPE, Robert
       Apostolike obedience. Shewing the Duty of
       Subiects to pay Tribute and Taxes to their
       Princes, according to the Word of God, in the
       law and the Gospell, and the Rules of Re-
       ligion, and Cases of Conscience... A Sermon
       Preached at Northampton, at the Assises, for
       the Countie, Febr. 22. 1626.
       London, printed by Miles Flesher, and are
       to be sold by Iames Bowler, 1627.
       4°. pp. [4], 1-36. STC 22526.

Abbot's refusal to license this sermon led to
his sequestration. The sermon was eventually
licensed by Monteigne, Bishop of London.

269   ENGLAND. Miscellaneous Public Documents
       The Commission to sequester Archbishop
       Abbot from all his ecclesiastical offices.

Appears in:

RUSHWORTH, John, M.A., compiler
Historical collections. [See no. 51.]
pp. 431-34.

It is also printed in such collections as
Frankland (no. 52), Wilkins (no. 251), Rymer
(no. 248), Cardwell (no. 37), An English
garner (no. 54), and Cobbett's State trials
(no. 53).

270   MAYNWARING, Roger
Religion and alegiance: in two sermons
preached before the Kings Maiestie, etc.
London, printed by I.H. for Richard
Badger, 1627.
4°. pp. [2], 1-56. STC 17751.

F   LOCAL CONNECTIONS

I   Surrey

For letters of 1614 and 1632 to the town
officials of Guildford, see nos. 66, 84, 85.
For a description of Abbot's Hospital and
its charter, etc., see no. 157.

271   HOBSON, John Morrison
          Some early and later houses of pity.
          London, Routledge, 1926.
          8°. pp. 199.

      pp. 136-50: "Abbot's Hospital".   Includes
      portrait, signature, views of Abbot's Hospital.

272   KING, Thomas William, <u>York herald</u>
          Remarks on a brass plate formerly in the
      Church of the Holy Trinity in Guildford, and
      now remaining in the hospital there. [On the
      plate to Maurice Abbot.]

      Appears in:

          SURREY ARCHAEOLOGICAL COLLECTIONS,
              Guildford, v. 3, 1865, pp. 254-66.

      Includes: Plate, facsimile of Abbot's signa-
      ture, funeral certificate of Abbot, entries
      in registers of Holy Trinity Church,
      genealogical table of Abbot's generation.

273   PALMER, Philip Griggs
          Archbishop Abbot and the woollen industry
      in Guildford.
          MS in **GuPL.**
          8°. ff. 66, a-g.

References on ff. a-g. Probably meant for
publication, many amendments having been made
to the MS.

274   PALMER, Philip Griggs
        The inventories of Abbot's Hospital, Guild-
      ford, 1709 ... [-]1825.

      Appears in:

          SURREY ARCHAEOLOGICAL COLLECTIONS, Guild-
            ford, v. 32, 1919, pp. 34-49.

      pp. 48-49: Abbot's plans for fostering the
      wool industry in Guildford and the endowment
      of Baker's Blue Coat School as Abbot's School
      with the money set aside for these plans once
      they had proved of no avail.

275   PALMER, Philip Griggs
        The Knight of the Red Cross: or, the
      romance of Archbishop Abbot's tomb, in the
      Church of the Holy and Undivided Trinity,
      Guildford, Surrey.
        Guildford, Lasham, 1911.
        8°. pp. 16. plates.

      On the figures of the canopy illustrating
      Abbot's life through use of the Legend of the
      Knight of the Red Cross (Faerie Queene, Book
      I). Transcribes inscriptions on monuments.

      No copy at L; copy seen at GuPL.

276   The VICTORIA history of the counties of
      England: Surrey. [Edited by H.E. Malden.]
        Westminster, Constable [etc.], 1902-14.
        4°. 4 vols. and index.

      References chiefly on Abbot and the woollen
      industry in Guildford and on buildings con-
      nected with Abbot.

II   Kent

For a letter to the Dean of Canterbury of
1630 concerning a font, see no. 86.

277   ARCHAEOLOGIA CANTIANA: being the transactions
of the Kent Archaeological Society.
      Canterbury, 1882-1915 passim.
      8°.

Collations to benefices made by Abbot passim
in vols. 14, 15, 16, 20, 21, 22, 25, 28, 31.

278   CLELAND, James, D.D.
        Iacobs Wel, and Abbots Conduit, paralleled,
preached, and applied (in the Cathedrall and
Metropoliticall Church of Christ in Canterbury) to the use of that citie; now to make
glad the Citie of God.
        London, printed for Robert Allot, 1626.
        4°. pp. [6], 1-53, [1]. STC 5395.

With an additional e.t.p. showing the conduit
and, as a frontispiece, a portrait of Abbot
by Passaens, with commendatory verses. The
work is dedicated to Abbot.

DEDICATIONS TO ABBOT

See also nos. 123, 189, 227, 234, 278.

This is based largely upon Williams' Index,
omitting some entries that were not strictly
dedications and two in which I could find no
dedications on examination of copies of the
books at O. John Field's Of the Church, 1628
edition, although listed in Madan as dedicated to Abbot, is omitted because the same
dedication remains in all editions from 1606
to 1635.

1610

279   BENEFIELD, Sebastian
      Doctrinae Christianae sex capita, etc.
      Oxoniae, excudebat Iosephus Barnesius,
      1610.
      4°. pp. [18], 1-208, [12]. STC 1867
      Madan i. 1610/1.

280   [DAVIES, John, of Hereford]
      The scourge of folly. Consisting of
      satyricall epigrams, and others in honour of
      many noble persons and worth friends, etc.
      At London printed by E.A. for Richard
      Redmer, 1610.
      8°. pp. [16], 1-264. STC 6341.

      p. 187: "To the right reverend Father in God,
      Doctor Abbot, Bishop of London." A sonnet.
      The preface signed I.D.

x281 DUNSTER, John
      Caesars penny, or a sermon of obedience
      ... Preached at St. Maries in Oxford at the
      Assizes the 24 Iuly 1610.
      At Oxford, printed by Ioseph Barnes, 1610.
      12°. pp. [6], 1-38, [4]. STC 7354;
      Madan i. 1610/3.

Not seen; entry copied from Madan.

1611

282   BANKES, Thomas, M.A.
          Celebris ad clerum concio, etc.
          Londini. Impressum per N. Okes, 1611.
          4°. pp. [8], 1-48. STC 1364.

To Abbot and Tobias Matthew, Archbishop
of York.

283   BOYS, John, Dean of Canterbury
          An exposition of the dominical Epistles
and Gospels, vsed in our English liturgie,
throughout the whole yeere...The summer-part,
etc.
          At London imprinted by Felix Kyngston,
for William Aspley, 1611.
          4°. pp. [4], 1-247, [1]. STC 3458.

The other parts are not dedicated to Abbot.
The dedication remains in the summer-part of
the 1615-16 edition, but not in editions of
this in Boys's works. Not at L; O copy seen.

284   CARLETON, George, Bishop of Llandaff
          and of Chichester
          Tithes examined and proued to be due to
the clergie by a diuine right... The second
edition, etc.
          At London: printed by Humfrey Lownes, for
Clement Knight, 1611.
          4°. pp. [8], 1-39, [1]. STC 4645.

The first edition was dedicated to Bancroft.

285   GARDINER, Samuel, D.D.
          The scourge of sacriledge.
          Imprinted at London by W.W. for Thomas Man,
1611.
          8°. A-M⁸. STC 11580.

Gardiner was chaplain to Abbot.

286   JAMES, Thomas, <u>D.D.</u>, <u>Sub-Dean of Wells</u>
          A treatise of the corruption of scripture,
       councels and fathers, by the prelates,
       pastors, and pillars of the Church of Rome,
       <u>etc</u>.
          At London, printed by H.L. for
       Mathew Lownes, 1611.
          4°. 5 pt. STC 14462.

       James was chaplain to Abbot. The dedication
       remains in the reissue of 1612 but is not in
       the 1688 edition.

287   SANDERSON, Thomas, <u>D.D.</u>, <u>Archdeacon</u>
             <u>of Rochester</u>
          Of Romanizing recusants, and dissembling
       Catholicks... An answer to the posthume
       pamphlet of Ralfe Bucklande, <u>etc</u>.
          At London, printed by Thomas Purfoot, 1611.
          4°. pp. [17], 2-99, [1]. STC 21711.

       Dedicated to the Lord Archbishop of Canter-
       bury; as it was entered in the Register in
       August 1611 this would be Abbot. Not at L;
       O copy seen.

288   SELLER, John
          A sermon against halting betweene two
       opinions, <u>etc</u>.
          London, printed by Thomas Creede for
       Ralphe Mabb, 1611.
          4°. pp. [8], 1-35 [i.e. 53], [1].
       STC 22182.

       Seller was chaplain to Abbot. Another issue
       was printed for William Welbie.

289   WILLET, Andrew
          Hexapla: that is, a six-fold commentarie
       vpon the most diuine Epistle of the Holy
       Apostle S. Paul to the Romanes, <u>etc</u>.
          [London,] Printed for Leonard Green
       (by Cantrell Legge), 1611.
          2°. 2 pt. STC 25690.

Part 2 only is dedicated to Abbot and
Andrewes. The dedication remains in the 1620
edition. Not at L; O copy seen.

1612

290   CHETWIND, Edward
          The strait gate, and narrow way to life.
       Opened, and pointed out in certaine sermons
       vpon Luke. 13. 23, 24, etc.
          London. Printed by William Hall, 1612.
       8°. pp. [32], 1-147, [3]. STC 5127.

       The dedication remains in the 1632 edition.
       Not at L; O copy seen.

291   COLLINS, Samuel
          Increpatio Andreae Eudaemono-Iohannis
       Iesuitae, de infami paralleo, et, renovata
       ascertio Torturae Torti, pro clarissimo
       Domino atque antistite Eliensi.
          Excudebat Cantrellus Legge, Inclytae
       Academiae Cantabrigiensis typographis, 1612.
       4°. pp. [16], 1-442. STC 5563.

292   MORNAY, Philippe de, Seigneur du Plessis-Marly
          The mysterie of iniquitie: that is to say,
       the historie of the Papacie... Englished by
       Samson Lennard.
          London: printed by Adam Islip, 1612.
       2°. pp. [20], 1-661, [1]. STC 18147.

       The dedication is by Lennard.

293   PAULE, Sir George
          The life of the most reuerend and religious
       prelate John Whitgift, Lord Archbishop of
       Canterbury.
          London: printed by Thomas Snodham, [1612].
       4°. pp. [4], 1-94. STC 19484.

       The dedication remains in the 1699 edition.

294 THOMPSON, Thomas
     Clauiger ecclesiae, seu concio ad clerum
de cauibus regni coelorum, habita pro forma,
Oxoniae in templo B. Mariae, die 16.
Februarij, 1610, etc.
     Londini, excudebat Richardus Field impensis
Nathanaelis Butler, 1612.
     8°. pp. [18], 1-152. STC 20913.

Not at L; O copy seen.

295 BOYS, John, Dean of Canterbury
     An exposition of the festiuall Epistles
and Gospels, vsed in our English liturgie ...
The first part from the Feast of S. Andrew
the Apostle to the Purification of Blessed
Mary the Virgin.
     At London imprinted by Felix Kingston, for
William Aspley. 1613.
     4°. pp. [4], 1-156. STC 3462.

The other parts are not dedicated to Abbot.
The dedication remains in later editions,
published both separately and in Boys's works.
L copy destroyed; LLP copy seen.

296 CARLETON, George, Bishop of Llandaff
        and of Chichester
     Consensus Ecclesiae Catholicae contra
Tridentinos, etc.
     Londini, in officina Nortoniana apud
Ioannem Billium, 1613.
     8°. pp. [22], 1-455, [1]. STC 4631.

297 DOWNAME, John
     Consolations for the afflicted: or, the
third part of the Christian warfare, etc.
     At London printed by Iohn Beale for
W. Welby, 1613.
     4°. pp. [36], 1-717, [1]. STC 7140.

The other parts are not dedicated to Abbot.
The dedication remains in the third part of
the fourth edition.

298   MASON, Francis, <u>Archdeacon of Norfolk</u>
        Of the consecration of bishops in the
      Church of England, <u>etc</u>.
        Imprinted at London by Robert Barker, 1613.
      2°. pp. [12], 1-269, [1]. STC 17597.

299   PURCHAS, Samuel
        Purchas his pilgrimage. Or relations of
      the world and the religions observed in all
      ages and places discovered, <u>etc</u>.
        London, printed by William Stansby, 1613.
      2°. pp.[28], 1-752, [20]. STC 20505.

      The dedication remains, with slight altera-
      tions, in later editions. Purchas became
      chaplain to Abbot in 1613.

300   WESTERMAN, William
        Iacobs Well: or, a sermon preached before
      the Kings ... Maiestie, <u>etc</u>.
        London, printed by Iohn Beale, for
      Matthew Lawe, 1613.
        8°. pp. [30], 1-80. STC 25281.

      Westerman was chaplain to Abbot. The dedica-
      tion remains in the 1616 edition.

301   WILLET, Andrew
        Synopsis Papisimi, that is a generall view
      of Papistrie... Now this fourth time perused
      and published, <u>etc</u>.
        At London, imprinted by Felix Kyngston,
      for Thomas Man, and are to be sold by Henry
      Fetherston, 1613.
        2°. pp. [24], 1-1352, [36]. STC 25699.

      The dedication is to part 1 only and is
      shared with John King, Bishop of London.
      It remains in the 1634 edition.

1614

302   BREREWOOD, Edward
      Enquiries touching the diuersity of
      languages and religions through the chiefe
      parts of the world.
      London, printed for John Bill, 1614.
      4°. pp. [24], 1-198. STC 3618.

      The dedication is by Sir Robert Brerewood and
      remains in later editions.

303   MAXWELL, James, M.A.
      Admirable and notable prophesies, vttered
      in former times by 24. famous Romain-
      Catholickes, etc.
      London, printed by Ed: Allde for Clement
      Knight, 1615.
      4°. pp. [20], 1-164, [2]. STC 17698.

      The dedication is shared with other bishops.
      Harvard UL has a fragment of a 1614 edition
      (Williams' Index).

304   PRIDEAUX, John, Bishop of Worcester
      Castigatio cuiusdam circulatoris qui R.P.
      Andream Eudaemon-Iohannem Cydonium e
      Societate Iesu nuncupet, etc.
      Oxoniae, excudebat Iosephus Barnesius,
      1614.
      8°. pp. [16], 1-179, 190-242, [16].
      STC 20344; Madan i. 1614/12.

305   REUTER, Adam
      Eadgarus in Iacobo rediuiuus seu Pietatis
      Anglicanae defensio, etc.
      Londini, 1614.
      4°. pp. [5], 2-30, [2]. STC 20913.

      Not at L; O copy seen.

1615

306   MASON, Thomas, Minister of Odiham
          Christs victorie ouer Sathans tyrannie,
      etc.
          London, printed by George Eld and Ralph
      Blower, 1615.
          2°. pp. [10], 1-418, [14]. STC 17622.

      Dedicated to Abbot and Sir Edward Coke.

1616

307   DILLINGHAM, Francis
          The probleme, propounded by Francis
      Dillingham, in which is plainely shewed, that
      the Holy Scriptures haue met with Popish
      arguments and opinions.
          London, imprinted by William Iones, and
      are to be sold by Ed. Weaver, [1616].
          8°. pp. [7], 2-42. STC 6887.

308   CHAMPNEY, Anthony
          A treatise of the vocation of bishops, and
      other ecclesiasticall ministers. Prouing the
      ministers of the pretended reformed churches
      in generall to haue no calling, etc.
          At Douay, by Iohn Heighem, 1616.
          4°. pp. [16], 1-326, [2]. STC 4960.

      To "Mr. George Abbat, called arch-bishop of
      Canterbury", and signed "Your seruant and
      frinde as you are Gods and His Churches".

309   GOSTWYKE, Roger
          The anatomie of Ananias; or, Gods censure
      against sacriledge, etc.
          Printed by Cantrell Legge, Printer to the
      Vniuersitie of Cambridge, 1616.
          4°. pp. [8], 1-183, [1]. STC 12100.

310   HAY, Peter
          A vision of Balaams asse. **VVherein** hee
      did perfectly see the present estate of
      the Church of Rome, etc.

London printed for Iohn Bill, 1616.
4°. pp. [24], 1-286. STC 12972.

311   HAYWARD, Sir John
       The sanctuarie of a troubled soule.
       London, printed by George Purslow, 1616.
       12°. pp. [58], 1-421, [1]. STC 13006.

The dedication remains in later editions.

312   NID, Gervase
       Certaine sermons vpon diuers texts of
       Scripture.
       London, printed by Nicholas Okes for
       Walter Burre, 1616.
       8°. pp. [6], 1-106. STC 18579.

313   SPEED, John, Historian
       A clowd of Vvitnesses: and they the holy
       genealogies of the sacred scriptures, etc.
       At London, printed by Iohn Beale for
       Daniell Speed, 1616.
       8°. ff. [8], 1-50, [38]. STC 23031.

The dedication remains in later editions.

314   SYLVESTER, Josuah, the Poet, editor and
           compiler
       The second session of the parliament of
       vertues reall ... for better propagation of
       all true piëtie, etc.
       [London, H. Lownes, 1616.]
       8°. 3 pt. STC 23582.

"Iob triumphant" and "A hymn of alms" are
dedicated to Abbot. The dedication remains
in editions of these works in Du Bartas's
Works, 1621, 1633, and 1641.

1617

315   ANTON, Robert
      Vices anotimie, scourged and corrected in
      new satirs.
      London, printed by Barnard Alsop for
      Roger Iackson, 1617.
          4°. 2 pt. STC 686.

      Part 2 is dedicated to Abbot.

x316 DELAUNE, Nathaniel
      The Christians tryumph. Manifested by the
      certitude of saluation, etc.
      London, printed by N.O. for Iohn Pyper,
      1617.
          8°. pp. [10], 1-86.

      Not at L or in STC. McAlpin Cat. entry copied.

317   DILLINGHAM, Francis
      Enchiridion Chrisianae [sic] fidei, ex
      patribus desumptum.
          Londini, excudebat Guilielmus Iones, 1617.
          8°. pp. [4], 1-106, [2]. STC 6884.

      Not at L; O copy seen.

1618

318   AIREY, Henry
      Lectures vpon the whole Epistle of St.
      Paul to the Philippians... Now published by
      C.P. [Christopher Potter]. [With the text.]
          London printed by Edw: Griffin for
      William Bladen, 1618.
          4°. pp. [20], 1-950. STC 245.

      The dedication is by Potter.

319   G., H.
      The mirrour of maiestie: or, the badges of
      honour conceitedly emblazoned: with emblems
      annexed, poetically vnfolded.

London, printed by William Iones, 1618.
4°. pp. [6], 1-63, [1]. STC 11496.

A poem to Abbot is on p. 8.

320   HULL, John
       An exposition vpon a part of the Lamenta-
tions of Ieremie: lectured at Corke, etc.
London, imprinted by Bernard Alsop, 1618.
4°. pp. [8], 1-349, [1]. STC 13931.

The dedication remains in the reissue of 1620
entitled Lectures vpon the Lamentations of
Ieremiah.

321   PILKINGTON, Richard
       Parallela: or, the grounds of the new
Romane Catholike, and of the ancient
Christian religion, out of the Holy Scripture
compared together, etc.
London. Printed for Iohn Bill, 1618.
4°. pp. [20], 1-416. STC 19933.

Not at L; O copy seen.

1619

322   ABBOT, Robert, Bishop of Salisbury
       De suprema potestate regia exercitationes
habitae in Academiâ Oxoniensi, contra Rob.
Bellarminum, & Francise. Suarez.
Londini, ex officina Nortoniana, apud
Iohannem Billium, 1619.
4°. pp. [18], 1-197, [1]. STC 47.

The dedication is by Thomas Abbot, the editor.

323   BRUYN, Ambrosius de
       In originem, vsum foedum, et ritum pro-
fanum, bacchanaliorum, Oratio, etc.
Londini, excudebat apud A.M., 1619.
4°. A-F⁴. STC 3951.

324   FOWNS, Richard
         Trisagion or, the three holy offices of
      Iesus Christ, the Sonne of God, priestly,
      propheticall, and regall, etc.
         London, Printed by Humfrey Lovvnes for
      Mathevv Lovvnes, 1619.
         4°. pp. [44], 1-346, [8], 347-782.
      STC 11216.

      Book 2 is dedicated to Abbot; its titlepage
      is dated 1618.

325   PETRUCCI, Lodovico
         Apologia equitis Ludouici Petrucci contra
      calumniatores suos, etc.
         Excusum Londini, 1619.
         4°. STC 19813.

      L and O copies have various collations.

      The dedication is to Abbot and Sir Francis
      Bacon.   There are also verses and an end-
      piece addressed to Abbot and others.

      1620

326   CHAMPNEY, Anthony
         Mr Pilkinton his Parallela disparalled.
      And the Catholicke Roman faith maintained
      against Protestantisme, etc.
         At S. Omers, for Iohn Heigham, 1620.
         8°. pp. [2], 3-220, [2]. STC 4959.

      To "Mr. George Abbat, called by some,
      Archbishoppe of Canturbury".

327   DAY, John, Vicar of St. Mary's Oxford, son of
                the printer
         Day's Descant on Dauids Psalms: or, a com-
      mentary vpon the Psalter, as it is usually
      read throughout the yeere... And first, of
      the first eight Psalmes, etc. [With the text.]
         Oxford, printed by Iohn Lichfield and
      Iames Short, 1620.
         4°. pp. [40], 1-222 [i.e. 220].
      STC 6424; Madan i. 1620/1.

328 HALL, Joseph, <u>Bishop of Exeter</u> and <u>of Norwich</u>
     The honor of the married clergie,
maintayned against the malicious challenge of
C.E. Masse-priest, <u>etc</u>.
     London, printed by W.S. for H. Fether,
1620.
     8°. pp. [24], 1-345, [27]. STC 12074.

The dedication remains in the 1628 and 1634
editions of Hall's works.

329 MAVERICKE, Radford
     Grieuing of Gods spirit, <u>etc</u>.
     London, printed by William Stansby, 1620.
     4°. pp. [5], 2-24. STC 17681.

Not at L; O copy seen.

330 JOHNSON, Robert, <u>B.D</u>.
     The way to glory: or, the preaching of
the Gospell is the ordinary means of our
Saluation, <u>etc</u>.
     London. Printed by Nicholas Okes, and are
to be sold by Iohn Pyper, 1621.
     4°. pp. [8], 1-45, [1].

Not at L or in STC; O copy seen.

     <u>1621</u>

331 MUSGRAVE, Christopher
     Musgraues motiues, and reasons, for his
secession and disseuering from the Church of
Rome and her doctrine, <u>etc</u>.
     At London, imprinted by F.K. for
Richard Moore, 1621.
     4°. A⁴(-A1), B-E⁴, F⁴ (-F4). STC 18316.

332 SLATYER, William
     The history of Great Britanie from the
first peopling of this Iland to this present
raigne, <u>etc</u>.
     London printed by W: Stansby, for Rich:
Meighen, 1621.
     2°. pp. [24], 1-303, [17]. STC 22634.

333   WITHER, George, the Poet
        The songs of the Old Testament, translated
      into English measures, etc.
        London, printed by T.S., 1621.
        12°. pp. [13], 2-72. STC 25923.

      The dedication is to all archbishops and
      bishops but mentions Abbot by name.

334   DOWNAME, John
        A guide to godlinesse, or a treatise of a
      Christian life, etc.
        Printed at London by Felix Kingstone for
      Ed: Weuer & W. Bladen, [1622].
        2°. pp. [36], 1-961, [1]. STC 7143.

      The dedication remains in the edition of 1629.

      1623

335   DU MOULIN, Pierre
        The Christian combate, or, a treatise of
      afflictions... Translated into English by
      Iohn Bulteel.
        London, printed by F.K. for Nathanaell
      Newbery, 1623.
        12°. pp. [48], 1-326, [2]. STC 7316.

      The dedication is by Bulteel. Not at L;
      LLP copy seen.

      1624

336   BARRELL, Robert
        The spirituall architecture, etc.
        Printed at London by Augustine Matthewes,
      and Iohn Norton, 1624.
        4°. pp. [8], 1-68. STC 1498.

337   FEATLEY, Daniel
        The Romish fisher caught and held in his
      owne net, etc.
        London, printed by H.L. for Robert
      Milbourne, 1624.
        4°. 3 pt. STC 10738.

Featley was chaplain to Abbot.

338   GEE, John, M.A.
      The foot out of snare: with a detection of
sundry late practices and impostures of the
priests and Jesuits in England, etc.
   London, printed by H.L. for Robert
Milbourne, 1624.
      4°. pp. [10], 1-99, [8]. STC 11701.

The dedication remains in later editions.

Reprinted in:

      SCOTT, Sir Walter, Bart., compiler
         A collection of... tracts. [See no. 41.]
      pp. 49-94.

339   HALL, Joseph, Bishop of Exeter and of Norwich
      Columba Noae oliuam adferens iactatissimae
Christi arcae, etc.
      Londini. Per Guil Stansby impensis
Guillelmi Barret, 1624.
      4°. pp. [6], 1-47, [1]. STC 12648c.

The dedication remains in editions of Hall's
works of 1628 and 1634.

340   MASON, Henry, Prebendary of St. Paul's
      The new art of lying, couered by Iesuites
vnder the vaile of equiuocation, etc.
      London: printed by George Purslowe for
Iohn Clarke, 1624.
      4°. pp. [20], 1-106. STC 17610.

The dedication remains in the 1634 edition.

1625

341   ANDREWE, George
      A quaternion of sermons preached in Ireland
in the summer season. 1624, etc.
      Dublin, imprinted by the Societie of
Stationers, 1625.
      4°. pp. [4], 1-107, [1]. STC 583.

The LLP copy is a presentation copy to Abbot
with a special dedication on leaf A4 cancel-
ling that to Viscount Falkland.

342   MARKHAM, Francis, <u>Muster-master of Nottingham</u>
       The booke of honour. Or, fiue decads of
       epistles of honour.
          London, printed by Augustine Matthewes,
       and John Norton, 1625.
          2°. pp. [8], 1-200. STC 17331.

       Epistle no. 2 of decad no. 1 "Honour diuine,
       aboue all honour" is to Abbot.

343   UDNY, Alexander
       A golden bell, and a pomegranate. A
       sermon preached at the visitation in Canter-
       bury. 7. of April. 1624.
          London, printed by A.M. and I.N. for
       Anthony Vphill, 1625.
          4°. A-F⁴. STC 24512.

344   WITHER, George, <u>the Poet</u>
       The schollers purgatory, discouered in the
       Stationers Common-wealth, <u>etc.</u>
          [London,] Imprinted for the Honest
       Stationers, [1625?].
          8°. pp. [9], 2-131, [1]. STC 25919.

       Addressed to the archbishops, bishops, and
       other members of Convocation.

       <u>1626</u>

345   PRYNNE, William
       The perpetuitie of a regenerate mans
       estate.
          London, printed for Michael Sparke, 1626.
          4°. pp. [46], 1-656. STC 20471.

       The dedication remains in later editions.

346 RYVES, <u>Sir</u> Thomas
    Imperatoris Iustiniani defensio aduersus
Alemannum.
    Londini, excudebat G. Stansbeius, 1626.
12°. pp. [10], 1-145, [1]. STC 21477.

The dedication remains in the Frankfort
edition of 1628.

1629

347 BURRELL, Percivall
    Sutton's synagogue or, the English
centurion, <u>etc</u>.
    Printed at London, by T.C. for Ralph Mabb,
1629.
4°. pp. [4], 1-25, [1]. STC 4126.

Dedicated to Abbot and all other governors of
"King James's Hospital", i.e. Christ's
Hospital. Another issue is undated.

1630

348 LORD, Henry, <u>Chaplain to the English Factory
    at Surat</u>
    A display of two forraigne sects in the
East Indies, vizt: the sect of the Banians
... and the sect of the Persees, <u>etc</u>.
    Imprinted at London for Francis Constable,
1630.
4°. 2 pt. STC 16825.

Part 2 is also dedicated to Sir Maurice Abbot.

1631

349 SMITH, John, <u>Governor of Virginia</u>
    Advertisements for the unexperienced
planters of New England, or any where, <u>etc</u>.
    London, printed by Iohn Haviland, and
are to be sold by Robert Milbourne, 1631.
4°. pp. [8], 1-40, [2]. STC 22787.

Dedicated to Abbot and Samuel Harsnett,
Archbishop of York.

1632

350   CAPELL, Moses
       Gods valuation of mans soule.
       London, printed by W.J. for Nicolas
Bourne, 1632.
       4°. pp. [14], 1-38. STC 4600.

1633

351   DOWNAME, George, Bishop of Derry
       A treatise of iustification.
       London, printed by Felix Kyngston for
Nicolas Bourne, 1633.
       2°. pp. [10], 1-660, [24]. STC 7121.

352   ROGERS, Francis, D.D.
       A visitation sermon, preached at the Lord
Archbishops triennial and ordinary visita-
tion, in St. Margarets in Canterbury vpon
Aprill the first, 1630.
       London, printed by Iohn Norton, for
William Adderton, 1633.
       4°. [A]². B-D⁴. STC 21176.

Not at L; O copy seen.

APPENDIX

PRINTED INDEXES AND CALENDARS

OF MANUSCRIPTS

* Denotes important volume or series.

A1: PUBLIC RECORD OFFICE

* 1] Calendar of state papers, domestic
     series ... preserved in ... Her
     Majesty's Public Record Office. Edited
     by Mary Anne Everett Green (and John
     Bruce, William Douglas Hamilton, and
     Sophia Crawford Lomas). 1601-1634 in
     11 vols., 1580-1649 addenda in 2 vols.
     1859-97.

  2] Calendar of state papers, colonial
     series [America and West Indies] ...
     preserved in the State Paper Department
     of Her Majesty's Public Record Office.
     Edited by W. Noel Stanley. 1574-1660 in
     1 vol., 1675-1676 and 1574-1674 addenda
     in 1 vol. 1860-93.

* 3] Calendar of state papers, colonial
     series, East Indies, China and Japan,
     preserved in Her Majesty's Public
     Record Office and elsewhere. Edited by
     W. Noel Sainsbury. 1513-1624 in 3 vols.
     1862.

  4] Calendar of state papers, colonial
     series, China and Persia, preserved in
     Her Majesty's Public Record Office and
     elsewhere. Edited by W. Noel Sainsbury.
     1625-34 in 2 vols.

* 5] Calendar of state papers and manu-
     scripts, relating to English affairs,
     existing in the archives and collec-
     tions of Venice, and in other libraries
     of Northern Italy ... Edited by Horatio
     F. Brown (and Allen B. Hinds). 1610-29

in 10 vols. 1905-15.

*   6] Acts of the Privy Council of England.
       1613-1629 in 12 vols. 1921-58.   In
       progress.

A2:   ROYAL COMMISSION ON HISTORICAL MANUSCRIPTS
      REPORTS

      The indexes and calendars in this series are
      given numbers according to the usual library
      numbering.

1-8,ii]   First(-ninth. Part II). report[s]
               of the Royal Commission on His-
               torical Manuscripts. 1874-1884.

*9,x,xii]   Calendar of the manuscripts of
               the Most Hon. the Marquis of
               Salisbury, preserved at Hatfield
               House. vols. 10, 17. 1904-38.

10]   Reports of the manuscripts of the
               Earl of Eglinton... C.S.H. Drum-
               mond Moray, etc. 1885. (10th
               Report. App. 1.)

12, iii]   Calendar of the manuscripts of
               the Dean and Chapter of Wells.
               v. 2. 1914. (10th Report.
               App. 3.)

18]   The manuscripts of the Corpora-
               tions of Southampton and King's
               Lynn. 1887. (11th Report.
               App. 3.)

22]   The manuscripts of the Duke of
               Leeds, the Bridgewater Trust,
               etc. 1888. (11th Report. App. 7.)

* 23,i]   The manuscripts of the Earl Cow-
               per preserved at Melbourne Hall.
               v. 1, index in v. 3. 1888.
               (12th Report. App. 1.)

24,i]   The manuscripts of His Grace the
               Duke of Rutland preserved at

Belvoir Castle. v. 1, index in
v. 2. 1888-89. (12th Report.
App. 4.)

29,iii,ix]   The manuscripts of His Grace the
Duke of Portland preserved at
Welbeck Abbey. Vols. 3, 9. 1894-
1923. (v. 3 is 14th Report.
App. 2.)

31]   The manuscripts of Rye ... Corporation, Captain Loder-Symonds
(John Dovaston), etc. 1892.
(13th Report. App. 4.)

35]   The manuscripts of Lord Kenyon.
1894. (14th Report. App. 4.)

* 36, i]   The manuscripts of the Marquis of
Ormonde, preserved at the Castle,
Kilkenny, v. 1. index. 1895-1909.
(v. 1 is 14th Report. App. 7.)

37]   The manuscripts of Lincoln, Bury
St. Edmunds, etc. 1895. (14th Report. App. 8.)

* 45,i,iii]   Report on the manuscript of the
Duke of Buccleuch & Queensberry,
preserved at Montagu House,
Whitehall. vols. 1, 3. 1899-1926.

51]   Report on the manuscript of F.W.
Leybourne-Popham of Littlecote,
Co. Wilts. 1899.

* 63]   Report on the manuscripts of Lord
Montagu of Beaulieu. 1900.

* 55,i,iii, viii]
Report on manuscripts in various
collections. vols. 1, 3, 8.
1901-14.

* 60,ii]   Supplementary report on the manu-
scripts of the Earl of Mar and
Kellie preserved at Alloa House
... Edited by Henry Paton. 1930.

62]   Report on the manuscripts of the
               Marquess of Lothian preserved at
               Blickling Hall, Norfolk. 1905.

63,i]   Report on the manuscripts of the
               Earl of Egmont, v. 1. 1905.

65]   Report on Franciscan manuscripts
               preserved at the convent, Mer-
               chants' Key, Dublin. 1906.

* 66]   Report on the manuscripts of the
               Earl of Ancaster, preserved at
               Grimsthorp. 1907.

* 71,i]   Report on the manuscripts of Alle
               Allen George Finch of Burley-on-
               the-Hill Rutland. v. 1. 1913.

72,1]   Report on the Laing manuscripts
               preserved in the University of
               Edinburgh. v. 1. 1914.

* 73]   Report on the records of the City
               of Exeter. 1916.

74]   Report on the Palk manuscripts in
               the possession of Mrs. Bannatyne
               of Haldon, Devon. 1922.

* 75,ii-iv]   Report on the manuscripts of the
               Marquis of Downshire, preserved
               at Easthampstead Park, Berks.
               vols. 2-4. 1939-40.

* 78,ii,iv]   Report on the manuscripts of the
               late Reginald Rawdon Hastings of
               the Manor House, Ashby-de-la-
               Zouche. Edited by Francis Bickley.
               v. 2. 1930.

80,i]   Calendar of the manuscripts of
               Lord Sackville preserved at Knole
               ... Edited by A.P. Newton. v. 1.
               1940.

A3:   BRITISH MUSEUM

* 1]   Catalogue of manuscripts in the
       British Museum. New series. v. 2.
       The Burney manuscripts. 1834.

* 2]   A catalogue of the Harleian manuscripts
       in the British Museum, etc. 4 vols.
       1808-12.

* 3]   A catalogue of the Lansdowne manu-
       scripts in the British Museum, etc.
       3 parts. 1812-19.

* 4]   Catalogue of the western manuscripts in
       the Old Royal & King's Collections. By
       Sir George F. Warner and Julius P.
       Gilson. v. 2, index in v. 3. 1921.

* 5]   Index to the Sloane manuscripts in the
       British Museum. By Edward J.L. Scott.
       1904. [For list see infra no. 7.]

* 6]   Catalogue of the Stowe manuscripts in
       the British Museum. 2 vols. 1895-96.

* 7]   A catalogue of the manuscripts pre-
       served in the British Museum hitherto
       undescribed ... Including the collec-
       tions of Sir Hans Sloane, Bart., Thomas
       Birch... By Samuel Ayscough. 2 vols.
       1782.

* 8]   List of additions to the manuscripts in
       the British Museum in the years 1836-
       1840 [and subsequent periods. Also in-
       cludes the Egerton manuscripts].
       13 vols. 1843-1959. In progress. Title
       varies. No reference in 1906-10, 1926-
       30 vols.

A4:   LAMBETH PALACE

* 1]   A catalogue of the archiepiscopal manu-
       scripts in the library at Lambeth
       Palace, with an account of the archi-
       episcopal registers and other records
       there preserved. 1812.

* 2]   Calendar of the Carew manuscripts pre-
       served in the archiepiscopal library
       at Lambeth. Edited by J.S. Brewer &
       William Bullen. v. 6. 1873.

A5:   OXFORD

* 1]   Catalogi codicum manuscriptorum Biblio-
       thecae Bodleianae. Pars Quarta. Codices
       viri admodum reverendi Thomae Tanneri,
       S.T.P. Episcopi Asaphensis complectens.
       Confecit Alfredus Hackman. 1860.

* 2]   Catalogi codicium manuscriptorum
       Bibliothecae Bodleianae. Partis Quintae.
       Viri munificentissimi Ricardi Rawlinson
       codicum classes duas priores (classem
       tertiam, classis quartae) complectens
       ... Confecit Gulielmus D. Macray.
       5 vols. 1878-1900.

* 3]   A descriptive, analytical and critical
       catalogue of the manuscripts bequeathed
       into the University of Oxford by Elias
       Ashmole...By William Henry Black. [Part
       10 of the quarto series.] 1 vol. and
       index. 1845-46.

* 4]   A summary catalogue of western manu-
       scripts in the Bodleian Library at
       Oxford which have not hitherto been
       catalogued in the quarto series...By
       Falconer Madan, H. H. E. Craster, N.
       Denholm-Young, (P.D. Record). vols. 2,
       ii, 3, 5, 6, 7. 1937-53.

* 5]   Catalogus codicum manuscriptorum qui in
       collegiis aulisque Oxoniensibus hodie
       adservantur. Confecit Henricus O. Coxe.
       2 vols. 1852. [Relevant manuscripts at
       Exeter, All Souls', and Corpus Christi
       Colleges.]

* 6]   Catalogue of the archives in the muni-
       ment rooms of All Souls' College.
       Prepared by Charles Trice Martin. 1877.

A6:   CAMBRIDGE

> A catalogue of the manuscripts
> preserved in the library of the
> University of Cambridge. 6 vols.
> 1856-67.

A7:   LICHFIELD

> Catalogue of the muniments and
> manuscript books pertaining to
> the Dean and Chapter of Lichfield.
> Compiled by J. Charles Cox. [c.1886.]

A8:   GENERAL REGISTER HOUSE, EDINBURGH

> The Register of the Privy Council
> of Scotland. Edited ... by David
> Masson. 1607-27 in 6 vols. 1887-99.

INDEXES

C SIXTEENTH- AND SEVENTEENTH-CENTURY PRINTERS
AND BOOKSELLERS NAMED OR IDENTIFIED FOR
SEPARATELY PUBLISHED WORKS BY ABBOT IN
SECTION A OF PART I
    (All in London unless otherwise stated)

Alsop, Bernard 14+, 14a+
Aspley, William, 26, 26a, 27, 27a
Barnes, Joseph (Oxford), 1, 23
Braddock, Richard, 5, 7
Bradwood, Melchisidech, 26, 26a, 27, 27a
Browne, John, 3-8
Field, Richard, 18, 18a, 19
Garbrand, Richard, 18a
Harper, Thomas, 11, 13+, 13a+
Judson, Thomas, 3, 4
Lichfield, John, 31
Lowndes, Humphrey, the Elder, 24, 24a, 24b
Marriot, John, 9, 10, 14+
Mathews, Augustine, 10, 25
Milbourne, Robert, 24, 24a, 24b, 25
Norton, John, 25
Playfere, John, 16+
Rosa, Jonah (Frankfort), 2
Scultetus, Abraham (Frankfort), 2
Sheares, Margaret, 16+
Sheares, William, 11, 12+, 13+, 13a+, 14+,
    14a+, 15+
Short, James, 31
Snodham, Thomas, 8, 9
Walkley, Thomas, 33
Waterson, Simon, 23
White, William, 6

+ Published after Abbot's death.